D.
Below 130 Feet

By Anton Swanepoel

A study on what it takes to do, and the effects of doing, deep dives

Diving Below 130 Feet

A study on what it takes to do, and the effects of doing deep dives

Reuben Watkins and Heidi Shappell
Divetech, Grand Cayman, Cayman Islands

www.antonswanepoelbooks.com
http://www.facebook.com/AuthorAntonSwanepoel

Anton Swanepoel

Introduction

Limits are only there as goal posts for us to find new ways to exceed them safely, so that we can set new limits. Diving is no exception to this age old truth.

One of the biggest perceived limitations in diving is depth. However, reaching any depth is not the problem, it is coming back that creates the problems, for even a rock can go to the bottom.

As with all limits set or perceived, there are facts and myths as to why it is a limit. When it comes to the depth limits in diving, there are more myths and misunderstandings than actual facts. Those that venture deeper are often seen as adventurers, heroes or crazy. However, the call of the deep will never go unanswered.

Welcome to deep diving

This book is about diving beyond 130 ft, the depth limit mostly accepted for recreational diving. Looking at why people dive deeper, the effects of pressure and gas on your body at depth, what it takes to dive deep, and what are the training options for deep diving. Additionally included are the effects of stimulants such as caffeine, smoking, diet, sugar, and more, on the human body while diving.

Note, this book is not a training manual for deep diving, however technical divers and divers interested in technical diving will find it of great value.

About the Author

Author at 200ft. Cayman Islands, Grand Cayman.
Photo taken by Robert Hew

At depth, correct training matters

Anton Swanepoel is a OC Tri-Mix instructor for IANTD, TDI and PADI and a NAUI instructor in addition to being a Tri-Mix gas blender and life support service technician instructor. He has a passion for wreck, cave and deep diving and has dove OC to over 400 ft.

Anton loves to research topics of interest to him and write about it. Our bodies and what happens to them underwater is a fascinating subject that we are only beginning to scratch the surface of in our research. This book is a collection of current knowledge regarding the effects of diving on the human body of investigations done on diving by offshore oil rigs, NASA, US Navy, Royal Navy, DAN, French Navy and a number of scientific research organizations.

Table of Contents

Anton Swanepoel

Anton Swanepoel

Chapter 1

How deep is deep?

Depth has always been a puzzling thing, for ask a non diver what is deep, and they might say 40 ft, while a Tri-Mix diver may say 300 ft. However, Emperor penguins can hold their breath for close to 30 minutes and dive to depths in excess of 1500 ft, and a northern elephant seal can hold its breath for almost two hours and dive to almost 5,000 ft. Deep therefore is relative and only a number. Thus deep is a number every diver needs to decide on for themselves, and that number may change as they gain experience. Officially deep is seen by many recreational agencies as either below 100 ft or 130 ft depending on the agency.

What is technical diving?

Interestingly, there is no universal agreement on the definition of technical diving. Some see it as diving below 130 ft (around 40 m), others when diving on mixtures other than air, while others see it as using equipment other than single open circuit (OC) gear, and others see it as doing overhead dives (either real as in caves or wrecks, or not real as in decompression diving). Thus technical diving is any of these, using gear other than single cylinder OC to do dives deeper or longer than recreational diving that could include overhead environments and possibly gasses other than air or recreation Nitrox (max 40 percent Oxygen in the mix).

Why dive deep?

People are strange creatures, we all want to do different things, yet when someone does something different than us or something we do not do, we want to know why. Then when reasons are given for their actions, we weigh their reasons up against our experience and values to see if they hold water, mostly not. We forget that our values and needs are different.

There are many reasons to go deeper, some are:
Exploring shipwrecks that are in deeper water.
Exploring cave or cave systems deeper.
For the pure enjoyment of going deeper.
To see fish or plant life only found deeper.
Commercial diving, like oil rigs.
Scientific diving, including research.
Searching for lost objects, including treasure hunting.
Salvaging cargo from sunken ships or crashed airplanes.
Ego.

However, there are actually only three main reasons that matter. You can, you want to, and because you want to be there.

-*You can*

Since diving deeper involves having more discipline and gear, it is not for every diver. Thus, those that venture deeper often pride themselves on being able to go deeper. Doing something few others can do, this can spur them on to go deeper and deeper in order to say that they are part of an ever shrinking number of elite people. Done right, they can become pioneers in setting new ways of going deeper, done incorrectly they can become just another statistic and can give deep diving a bad name.

-*You want to*

Wanting to go deeper is almost like the reason for you can, however it differs in one area, ego. Diving deeper just to say you can is mostly to impress other divers. However, diving deeper because you like the gear, the preparation, the discipline of the dive, the feeling of being alive and the knowledge that few if any divers have gone where you now are, is a path to finding yourself.

It is personal, and few of these divers even comment to others about the depths they go. It is not so much that they do not care what others think, but more, that they realize they are different and that they would much rather spend their money and time on diving deep than other things. They have heard so many excuses as to why they should not go deeper from many people that know very little about diving, that they need not explain themselves to those that would never understand them or their reasons.

-*You want to be there*

Interestingly this is one of the biggest reasons to go deeper, and it is the same reason why people go diving. You do not go diving to see fish, wrecks or other stuff. For you can see those in books and films. You go diving to actually be there with them, be in the wreck or cave, be next to a turtle or manta ray. The divers going deeper or in caves and wrecks just have a different be there place than divers doing 40 ft dives on a reef, however the reason still remains the same, to be there. No matter if you are doing deep saturation diving or deep bounce diving (even 3 hours at 330 ft is short compared to a deep multi week saturation dive) you are still choosing to be there.

The adventure

Diving by itself is an adventure, however deep, wreck, cave and decompression diving takes adventure to new limits.

No matter if you are deep in a cave or a wreck or below 400 ft in open water, it's a feeling one cannot really describe, you have to feel it for yourself. The knowledge that your time there is limited, your gas supply is limited, your life is limited, you stare death calmly in the eyes. It is not about thrill seeking, but the choice to live. When you know exactly how short your life will be if you do not go up, when you have the chance to just let it go, but decide to come back (sometimes even fighting), you appreciate life so much more.

After a deep dive, you look at the world differently, you hear people complain about the toothpaste cap, or the toilet seat, you see people argue or get upset about the smallest things, and you know you chose to come back to it all. You start to become larger than life, for you fear death less and accept it.

The risk

Every dive, not only deep ones, carry a degree of risk. In deep diving the risk is normally thought to be higher than recreational divers and to an extent this is true. A dive to 400 ft does have more risk than a dive to 40 ft. However, take for instance a new diver with four dives in total that then does a boat dive off the Caribbean wall to 100 ft. The diver has one first-stage regulator and one BCD bladder with very limited experience; compare that dive to a diver on double tanks with two first-stage regulators and a double bladder BCD system that has hundreds of dives - who is more at risk?

On the other hand, what is safe? For no dive is without risk. Although one may calculate to a degree the percentage of risk for say DCS, lost at sea and other hazards to which the diver is exposed, in the end it is up to the diver to accept the risk of not coming back, no matter the depth of the dive. However, all divers should have the reserve mental and physical ability to cope with emergencies at depth, no matter the depth.

Two kinds of deep divers

There are two kinds of deep divers, the explorers and the adventure seekers.

-Adventure seekers

Adventure seekers are only in it for the thrill of it, there is little thought of safety but just the number on their computer that they can brag with after the dive. Although they may have survived the dive, the chances of doing it again on the profile and equipment used is minimum, however that does not bother them since they have done it and can now brag about it. For instance, a dive to 200 ft (60 m) on a single air tank with recreational gear is purely adrenaline and adventure seeking.

-Explorers

Explorers are not just out to seek a number on their computers; they try to find safe ways to reach the depths they go to that are not only repeatable but also teachable. Thus, they carve a new path that will allow others to follow in their footsteps and maybe even surpass them. The explorer uses the ways they did previous deep dives and constantly improves on them to slowly push deeper and deeper with procedures that are repeatable, not one of luck dives. For instance, the Woodville Karst Plain Project (WKPP) divers, slowly pushing diving deeper and deeper while continually improving their methods.

Last thought on deep diving

Diving deep, as with so many things in life, can only truly be understood by those that share the same passion.

Anton Swanepoel

Chapter 2

Evolution of diving

Venturing beneath the surface of the water is still just as exciting today as it was for the pioneers of diving. We know more about distant stars and galaxies than we know about what lies in the deep dark waters of our oceans. Following is a short look at interesting events in the progress of underwater exploration.

-First breath-hold divers

The first breath-hold divers whom we have found evidence of dates back to 4500 B.C., and from the vast number of mother-of-pearl ornaments discovered in Egypt dating back to the Theban VI Dynasty in 3200 B.C. clearly diving was widespread. However, the Greek sponge divers stand out from others due to their success in exploring deeper and deeper depths to recover sponges. Documents exist that show organized large-scale pearl diving in 550 B.C. in India and Ceylon, and in Japan the AMA divers have been diving even before Christ. The first recorded use of divers for war was in the Trojan wars (1194 to 84 B.C.), and it is thought that these divers sabotaged enemy ships by cutting their anchor lines and drilling holes in the bottom of the ships. Even the Vikings used this method of sinking enemy ships, it is recorded that in the year 1000 a group of Swedish Vikings sank 16 Danish ships in this way.

Today however, breath-hold diving is more a sport and leisure past time, as many pearl and sponge divers now use modern diving gear.

-First diving bell

The first diving bell reported to have been used was by Alexander the Great in 332 B.C. during an attack on an island stronghold of Tyre. It is reported that Alexander used divers to attach the port blockades and descended in a container to watch the attack underwater. Aristotle mentioned a device used in 360 B.C. that supplied sponge divers with additional air, and although the diver was not in the device as Alexander was, it shows the use of mechanical means to extend a diver's time underwater is not relatively new to us. Although it is logical to assume that these underwater air containers and diving bells were used continuously after Alexander, no mention is made of diving bells until 1531 where a bell was used in Lake Nemi (near Rome) to locate two galleys of Emperor Caligula's that sank.

The catalyst for the diving bell construction however came from two Greek designers in 1538 that demonstrated their diving bell (the Toledo diving bell) to Emperor Charles V and thousands of spectators.

This bell was large enough that the inventor could sit inside the bell. A candle was placed inside the bell to give illumination underwater, in addition to being good showmanship. One can imagine the king's surprise to see the candle still burning when the bell was raised from the water after its dive.

However, it was not until 1689 that diving bells improved by being supplied by surface air. Up to this point bell diving was limited to the amount of air the bell held, and it needed to be raised when either the air was used up or the heat in the bell became too much to bear due to the diver's breathing.
Dr. Denis Papin, a French physicist, invented a way to supply diving bells with fresh air from large bellows on the surface. Unfortunately, the idea did rely on very unreliable bellows at the time and did not work properly until 1788 when John Smeaton, an English engineer, invented reliable pumps. Until Smeaton's invention, a diving bell invented by Edmund Halley (astronomer known for the comet Halley) was also in use. This bell used a lead cask that contained fresh air and was lowered into the water where the diver could continuously refresh the air in the bell with additional casks being lowered down.

-First diving helmets

Halley also invented a helmet which had a flexible hose connected to it and held in the bell. This allowed the range of the diver to be increased as divers normally had to hold their breath outside the bell and needed to return constantly to get fresh air. An English inventor named Becker invented a diving suit in 1715 made of leather with a metal helmet that was supplied with fresh air from the surface. Various other inventors followed the design and many improvements were made over the years. The best known is from an English inventor called Augustus Siebe (also called the father of helmet diving). His invention had a brass helmet with a leather suit. Unlike other suits that fully enclosed the diver, this one only half covered the diver. Due to this design a diver had to be upright else the suit would flood. Siebe did change the design in 1837 to make his suit watertight, in addition to adding a manual exhaust vent that allowed the diver to increase the air pressure in the suit to compensate for water pressure, eliminating suit squeeze.

By the 1800s diving bells were common in most large ports around Europe, these bells were not only used for dock building, ship repair and pier construction but also for sight seeing in some places. One famous tourist was Archduke Maximilian in 1818 where he picked up a stone as a souvenir from the bottom on his visit to England.

-The Caisson bell

The 'caisson' bell was invented in 1788 by John Smeaton and was a huge cast iron bell that could hold up to 12 workmen. This was invented originally for the building of the Eddystone Lighthouse on the treacherous 'Eddystone', United Kingdom. Due to extreme sea conditions, the lighthouse had to be rebuilt as the first two were destroyed and the third (known as Smeaton's Tower) was badly damaged, its upper portion was re-erected as a monument in Plymouth. Smeaton's Tower is also historically important as it changed the way lighthouses were designed and built, due to it showing the importance of concrete for building lighthouses.

The 'caisson' bell used improved pumps that would continuously supply the workers with fresh air to extend their bottom time, in addition to keeping water out of the bell. By the 1840s, the 'caisson' bell became standard use for most large underwater projects such as harbors and other long-term projects.

The bell was by now a massive long block and did not resemble the kettle or bell-shaped design of before, in addition to now allowing workers to live in the bell for days at a time. However, this caused serious cases of decompression sickness that were not understood at the time (and are still not totally understood today).

-The Era of the helmet

By 1850, the original diving bells became obsolete as diving helmets supplied with fresh air from pumps on the surface replaced them. The diving helmet allowed the diver to move around more freely and did not need the large cranes diving bells needed. The risk was also lower for helmet diving, as in rough seas diving bells could turn over and drown the divers. Helmet diving is common today not only in commercial and scientific diving but also by search and rescue workers and sometimes police. The hose that connects the diver to the surface is called an umbilical cord and has a gas supply hose and a communications line. A problem with umbilical diving is that if the pumps fail, the diver is not only starved of air, but the pressure in the helmet would lessen, and at depth the water pressure would be enough to crush a diver's body into a pulp in the diving helmet. Myth busters did an excellent episode with graphical scenes where a simulated diver's body made of a pig carcass was pushed up into the helmet and the gas hose.

Due to this problem a safety return valve was added to diving helmets after some deaths occurred. Divers are also now supplied in most cases with a bailout bottle that gives them a limited supply of gas they can independently switch to until a safety diver can reach them.

-First scuba units

Although there have been many designs to try to allow divers to remain underwater without the need to be supplied with fresh air from the surface, the first workable self-contained underwater breathing unit (SCUBA) was invented in 1825 by an Englishman, William James. James's design used a cylindrical belt that was wrapped around a diver's trunk, serving as an air reserve with an air pressure of around 450 psi, however if the unit was fully used is not known. In 1865, mining engineer and Navy Lieutenant Auguste Denayrouze invented a semi SCUBA unit. The unit had a metal cylinder on the diver's back that was pressurized to 40 ata from pumps on the surface. The diver could disconnect the hoses and function for a limited time on the reserve in the tank. The unit also had a regulator that used a membrane to work and responded to outside pressure to regulate the pressure at which the diver breathed gas, and also only worked on demand (when the diver inhales) to conserve air.

In 1900 French professor of biology, Louis Boutan of Algiers University designed a scuba unit which had a cylinder with compressed air of sufficient volume to sustain him for three hours at 70 ft. Although it was used extensively by him for underwater photography, he did not advertise his unit or put it into production. In 1933 Le Prieur started making SCUBA units that had a tank of compressed air on the diver's back with a hose leading to a diving mask. A valve allowed the diver to control airflow into the mask as needed and could provide a diver with enough air to last 10 minutes at 40 ft. In 1935 the French Navy adopted his design and in 1936 the first scuba diving club 'Club of Divers and Underwater Life' was formed. Interestingly, in all the time up to 1942, Lieutenant Auguste Denayrouze's regulator was ignored by all designers until Jacques Cousteau and Emile Gagnan reintroduced it in their design using Le Prieur's compressed air cylinder design together with Denayrouze's regulator.

The new unit allowed divers to descend to depths not capable of before, and in October 1943 Frederic Dumas reached 220 ft, followed by 307 ft in August 1947. A few weeks after Dumas' dive, Maurine Fargues a French Naval officer lost his life on a 397 ft dive upon returning to the surface (thought to be due to CNS DCS). Cousteau continually improved his unit (called the Aqualung), and his design forms the basis for modern SCUBA gear.

-First CCR unit

The oldest known patent for a rebreather comes from 17 June 1808 by Sieur Touboulic from Brest, called Ichtioandre, Greek for 'fish-man'. He was a mechanic in Napoleon's Imperial Navy and designed an Oxygen rebreather, although it is unclear if the design did go into production.

The design was simple with Oxygen being replaced manually by the diver from a reservoir. The gas circulated a closed loop and CO2 was removed by a sponge scrubber that was soaked in lime water. In 1849 a chemist, Pierre-Aimable de Saint Simon Sicard, designed and built the first practical Oxygen rebreather and demonstrated it in London in 1854.

In 1876 Englishman and merchant seaman, Henry A. Fleuss developed a practical CCR unit which is the forerunner of modern CCR units. This unit used rope soaked in caustic soda to remove CO2 from the loop and gave a bottom time of around three hours. This unit was made famous by an English diver called Alexander Lambert in 1880 when he entered a flooded tunnel to seal a hatchway door that was located in 60 ft of water and 1000 ft back into the tunnel. This rebreather was also used in a modified version from 1900 to 1910 as a submarine escape device as O2 toxicity was not thought to be a problem if a diver ascended quickly to the surface even from several hundred feet.

-Modern diving

Today diving bells are again in use, but have undergone massive changes to the original design, including being sealed with normally a double hatch that allows divers to enter and exit the bell through a smaller compartment where divers can don and doff diving gear as needed. These bells are mostly used in commercial work and deep saturation diving. Habitats where workers live for sometimes months at a time are also used in deep saturation diving. Scuba units are also employed both in commercial and non commercial fields. Although rebreathers are not used much in commercial deep diving, they are used extensively for search and recover, research and technical divers.

-Armored diving suits

Due to the limitations imposed on helmet divers (time at bottom and depth) a new approach was tried where the diver is in a suit that protects the diver from the water pressure, almost like a one-man submarine.

However, unlike a submarine, the armored suit allows a diver full movement as a helmet diver would, without the worry of decompression sickness as the pressure in the suit is the same as on the surface.

The first armored diving suit was designed by Englishmen W. H. Taylor in 1838 and was capable of reaching 150 ft, where helmet divers of the time were only able to reach 100 ft. Improvements to the suits from a number of designers allowed divers to reach 300 ft by 1900. Modern diving suits are capable of reaching depths of over 3000 ft.

Even though the armored suit may sound like an ideal replacement for helmet divers, it has a few drawbacks. One is that the earlier models were very heavy and did not allow divers much movement on the bottom. Later models did however have significant weight reduction, and in-water weight was in the range of 75 lbs. However, the second drawback was and still is the limiting factor of its use today, cost. Armored diving suits are very expensive to build and maintain, in addition to the risk that should the suit leak the diver normally drowns due to the suit flooding.

Some new armored suits have self-propulsion systems, normally electric driven screws (propellors), which allow it more freedom of movement underwater. The primary role of armored diving suits is for deep dives where remote operating vehicles cannot enter or do not have the dexterity for the job, in addition to very long dives that would make helmet diving impractical.

Armored suits are sometimes called JIM suits (named after Jim Jarratt that used the forerunner suit to dive to 500 ft searching for 'Nessy' in Lock Ness) or one atmosphere suits (due to the diver remaining at one atmosphere pressure).

-Submarines

An Englishman, William Bourne, is the first recorded designer of a prototype submarine in 1578, although the plans never left the drawing boards. It was not until 1605 that Magnus Pegelius designed and built the first submarine, which unfortunately became buried in mud on a dive. In 1620 Dutchman Cornelius Jacobszoon Drebbel, who was in the service of King James I, built two successful submarines propelled by oars and made of wood, capable of descending to 12 ft. For 10 years he used them as a tourist attraction on the Thames and it is reported that even King James I made an underwater trip.

As is the case of all new things, their military use was not long in being discovered, and in 1776 the first military submarine (designed by American David Bushnell) called 'Turtle' was launched. The submarine was hand-powered and in the shape of an egg, and was the first submarine documented and verified to be capable of independent underwater operation in addition to being the first to use screws for propulsion. It is documented that on September 7, 1776 Sgt. Ezra Lee from the Continental Army tried and failed to sink the British warship HMS Eagle during the American Revolutionary War while she was in New York harbor.

The first dual propulsion submarine was the Nautilus in 1800, built in France and designed by Robert Fulton. The submarine was human powered, in addition to having a sail for surface propulsion.

The French submarine Plongeur (launched 1863) was the first submarine not to rely on human power for propulsion by having a reciprocating engine powered by compressed air from 23 tanks at 180 psi. In 1867 the converted human-powered submarine Ictineo II, designed by Narcís Monturiol, was the first combustion driven submarine, using peroxide and steam propulsion. The sub was capable of diving to around 100 ft (30 m). The chemical process used for underwater propulsion released Oxygen into the submarine that replenished the crew's supply. Later, diesel-electric power would dominate submarine propulsion until the invention of nuclear-powered submarines (1950).

Today military submarines are capable of being submerged for days on end and are capable of diving to 3366 ft (1020 m). However, submarines are not only used for military purposes today, but also for research, tourism and drug and gun smuggling.

Chapter 3

Training for deeper diving

A world-renowned violin player was once approached by a lady who said that she wished she could play as well as he did. She said that she would give up anything to be able to play like him. His response was that he did, he told her that he practiced every day for multiple hours. Her response was 'Oh no, I do not want to practice, I just want to play the violin.'

Why Train for deeper diving?

It is common to hear divers talk about going to 160 or even 200 ft on a single air tank. Bragging on how cool they are, few realize how close they may have come to injury or death.

Going outside of recreational limits requires a different way of diving, thinking, planning and diver attitude.

When you plan a recreational dive, you plan to go diving. Very little thought is given to contingency. Plans are normally basic like 'we will turn around at half tank or close to it'. It is not that the diver is slack, the environment is just different. If your BCD malfunctions, you are low on gas, your mask breaks, you lose a fin, your regulator free flows, you get lost, and many more things that can happen, you just surface and end the dive.

On technical dives you normally do not have the option of just surfacing when things go wrong, thus you need to plan your dive to come back alive. New solutions need to be found and learned for every problem that can occur where you would normally just have surfaced.

For example, by taking a spare mask you will be able to continue your dive should your main mask break, and a free flowing regulator will be shut down to save gas.

Each problem now needs a specific solution to that problem, not just a general solution for all problems like surfacing and ending the dive.

These new skills can only be successfully learned and practiced under the guidance of a qualified technical instructor. Remember learning is both knowledge and experience. Knowledge is knowing what to do, experience is doing it.

Due to the risk of injury and death increasing the deeper you go down, so does the training and skill level for each course you take increase. It is a step by step process and you proceed to the next level once you have mastered the previous level.

Many divers ask if they can do a try Tri-Mix dive, just to see what it is like at 330 ft. However, they are not interested in learning to go that deep, and some are not even divers at all. That would be like walking up to Ferrari and asking them to let you compete in the next formula one grand-prix race because you would like to experience how it feels to race a formula one car, however you do not have a driver's license yet, nor have you ever driven a car.

Only by taking the correct training and going step by step deeper, can you gain the knowledge and experience to do the dives, including the appreciation of the dangers and disciplines involved in this type of diving.

Where to train

Knowing that you need training is only half of it, you now need to put your desires into action. Although there are a multitude of training agencies offering training in technical diving, they mostly follow the same steps of progression.

The following is a general guideline of the steps, check with your instructor as to the specific requirements for the agency he/she trains in.

Logically, your first step would be your entry level diver certification. Normally called open water, scuba diver, one star diver or first level. Note that you can start diving on rebreathers without first doing open circuit training, however it is not advised due to the cost and dedication involved in diving rebreathers. Most entry level certifications train you to dive to 60 ft (18 m) and you normally do four to five dives to complete the training.

After completing your entry level certification your next step would be advanced diver or two star diver. This would be your second-level diver. Most training agencies qualify you to dive to 100 to 130 ft (30 to 40 m) at this level. Here you normally learn new skills for navigation, night or low visibility diving, deeper diving and additional areas of interest like digital photography or DPV (diver propulsion vehicle) diving. The course is normally completed in five to eight dives.

There are two specialty ratings in recreational diving that you need to complete before you can enter technical diving. These are enriched air (Nitrox) and deep specialty diver. However, it is possible to combine the training of these courses into the first level technical training course if enough time is available.

First level technical training

After completing your Nitrox and deep diver rating, your first step is Advanced Nitrox (Adv EANx) and Decompression procedures diver. Note that some agencies like IANTD combine these two into one course just called Advanced Nitrox diver. You normally need around 20 to 25 dives in total to start this course. PADI currently has the TEC Deep diver course that can be done in one session called Tec Deep, or three sessions, called TEC 40 (40 m depth no deco) TEC 45 (45 m depth with limited deco) and TEC 50 (50 m depth with deco). There is an option to take Helium training with these classes, resulting in a light Tri-Mix qualification.

Tec Deep or Adv EANx is your first step and forms the basis for all your training to follow. Depending on the agency, this level allows you to dive to between 140 to 165 ft (42 to 50 m) on EANx (enriched air Nitrox, x = %O2) mixes up to pure Oxygen (O2). It trains you how to plan for decompression dives using EANx or Oxygen for accelerated decompression, with the focus on gas calculation and contingency planning. This course is also a requirement for most rebreather courses that involve decompression diving, you can however combine the Adv EANx class with a rebreather class.

After completing your Adv EANx class or Tech diver in PADI, you can either move on to deep air or light Tri-Mix or straight on to deeper Tri-Mix.

Deep air, extended-range diver or technical diver

Although the name differs from agency to agency, the end result is basically the same. This rating allows you to dive to 180 ft (54 m) on air, with accelerated decompression on EANx mixes or Oxygen.

Although you can skip this course and go on to Tri-Mix directly, this course does have its place. In some parts of the world Nitrox is hard to come by, let alone Tri-Mix. Deep air dives are basically the only cost-effective way of diving. However, due to the high level of narcosis the diver needs to tolerate, not everyone can or wants to do the course.

Anton Swanepoel

Recreational and Advanced Recreational Tri-Mix

This course is an entry level Tri-Mix course. It allows the diver to dive to 160 ft on Tri-Mix, provided that the END (equivalent narcotic depth) does not exceed 80 ft. At the advanced level the diver can plan and dive limited decompression dives. This is more for divers who want to go deeper without the effects of narcosis without going to the full extent of Tri-Mix training. Note that if a diver elected to incorporate Helium training while taking the PADI TEC 45 or 50 programs, then it is basically the same rating as Adv Rec Tri-Mix.

Tri-Mix or Normoxic Tri-Mix

Tri-Mix (TDI) and Normoxic Tri-Mix (IANTD) allows you to dive with mixes containing Helium to reduce narcosis , so long as the mix still contains an Oxygen percentage of 20% (18% for TDI) or higher. *'Normoxic'* thus means normal Oxygen as the mix must contain an Oxygen percentage close to normal air (21%) or higher, thus Normoxic Tri-Mix allows you to dive to max 200 ft (60 m) on 20% and 220 ft (66.7 m) for 18% O2 mix, as this is where the O2 partial pressure will reach 1.4 ata or close to it.

The diver will normally carry one to two cylinders for their back gas in addition to decompression cylinders slung on the side. A normal back gas for this level is around 20/35, a mix containing 20% Oxygen and 35% Helium. A lighter Tri-Mix of say 40/20 can be used as a travel mix with a final decompression mix of EAN50, EAN80 or O2.

Advanced Tri-Mix or Tri-Mix

The next step in your training will be Advanced Tri-Mix (TDI) or just Tri-Mix (IANTD and PADI). Here the diver is trained on how to use hypoxic mixes and dive to 330 ft (100 m). Due to the Oxygen in the mix becoming toxic at depths below 220 ft (66.7 m) on normal Oxygen content (21%) mixes, the percentage of Oxygen needs to be lowered to a level that is safe to breath at depth. However, this gas has an Oxygen content so low that should the diver breath it on the surface, he/she could pass out from lack of Oxygen (Hypoxia). Depending on the diver's surface air consumption (SAC) rate and planned bottom time, the diver may carry from two to four or more side tanks in addition to his/her back gas.

At this level it is common for divers to use a travel gas on descent and ascent. A travel gas is a gas that is breathable from the surface down to a depth where it is safe to breath from the back gas or another travel gas.

Expedition Tri-Mix

At the time of writing, only IANTD offers this course. This is an extreme diving course and is meant more for divers doing expedition dives rather than depth. However the course does train and qualify the diver to dive to 400 ft (121 m).

Chapter 4

Rebreather vs open circuit

In the left corner we have the defending champion, open circuit, weighing in at a hefty twins and multiple tanks, and in the right corner we have the challenger, rebreather, lighter with fewer tanks.

For every job, there is a tool, and sometimes there is more than one tool for the same job. One will be perfect, the other just ok.

Due to divers being able to do technical training for either open or closed circuit, one could ask which training is right for my needs?

Open circuit

Open circuit diving is by far the most common type of diving found today. Gas is compressed into cylinders and normally carried on the diver's back or sides. The pressures in the cylinders are normally in the range of 2400 to 4500 psi. Due to the pressure being too high for the diver to breathe, a reduction in pressure is needed. This is done in two steps (unless it is an old one piece regulator). The first step is to reduce the pressure in the tank to a pressure of around 120 to 150 psi (8 to 10 bar) above ambient pressure, consequently the item is called the first stage. The second reduction is done by, jup, the second stage. Here the gas pressure is reduced to just over ambient pressure.

As the diver descends deeper, the regulator will keep on adjusting the pressure to match the ambient pressure. Every time the diver breathes in, a valve opens in the second stage until the diver stops inhaling. When the diver exhales, the gas is directed to an exhaust port where it is expelled into the water. Due to the diver only needing a portion of the Oxygen that is contained in the gas with every breath, a lot of gas is lost. On the surface we use roughly 4 to 6% of the 21% Oxygen found in air.

Rebreather

Although the technical workings of a rebreather or CCR (closed circuit rebreather) unit are very involved and differ from unit to unit, the basic workings are relatively easy to understand.

A CCR unit will have two small cylinders, normally 13 to 20 cu ft in size. One cylinder is filled with pure Oxygen while the second is filled with a diluent gas, being normally air, Tri-Mix, Helair or Heliox. One or two breathing bags are attached to a canister holding a scrubber material. The diver starts by adding diluent to the unit until he/she can comfortably breathe at depth.

Gas from the inhalation bag is inhaled by the diver and on exhalation one way valves let the gas flow into the exhale bag (unless only one bag is used to perform both functions (normally back mounted counter lung)). The gas that was in the exhale bag is pushed out into the scrubber canister. Here the scrubber material undergoes a chemical reaction with the CO_2 in the exhaled gas and scrubs the gas clean of CO_2.

The gas then flows past from one to four Oxygen sensors that measure the left-over amount of Oxygen in the gas. An on-board computer calculates the amount of Oxygen that is required to replace the used Oxygen and triggers a solenoid that allows Oxygen to flow from the Oxygen cylinder into the loop. The gas then moves to the inhalation bag where the diver then inhales the recycled gas.

Thus, the diluent is only used to give volume to the bags allowing the diver to breathe and to dilute the Oxygen. Once the diver has added enough diluent to the unit to allow him/her to breathe comfortably at a depth, only gas from the Oxygen cylinder is needed (as long as the diver stays at the same depth). Since metabolism is not affected much by depth, the gas consumption is therefore the same regardless of how deep the diver dives, unlike open circuit where the divers use more gas as the depth increases.

Breathing resistance differs between OC and CCR, and even between different CCR units. How many counter lungs (two or one) and where they are located (back, front or shoulder mounted) affect the breathing resistance on CCR units, including the position of the diver in the water (horizontal or vertical). Although diver position does affect OC divers to a degree, it is normally negligible when compared to CCR divers. The CCR diver actually drives the gas volume around; his/her lungs are the pump that pushes gas into the counter lung(s) and through the CO_2 absorption material, all of these cause resistance.

The OC diver only needs to pull enough against the regulator diaphragm to open it, thereafter the regulator supplies gas to the diver at a pressure slightly above ambient pressure, making it easier to inhale. On the exhale the OC diver has the resistance of the regulator and water. All in all, the OC diver has less resistance in breathing than the CCR diver; this becomes exponential the deeper the diver dives due to the gas density increasing with depth. At extreme depths, below 500 ft (150 m) (possibly shallower if low percentages of Helium are used in the mix) the diver may have difficulty breathing, especially if the diver exerts him/herself due to work, current or other exertion tasks.

An additional thought in gas resistance is the design of CCR hoses, many of them have spirals in the hose to help against collapse due to the pressure. The spiral design also makes the hoses more flexible, a feature needed on the unit as the diver will be moving his/her head around during the dive. Non flexible hoses would have made this very difficult. However, the thought is that these rings cause gas restriction due to the natural rise and fall of the contour of the hose interior. Basically like a river bank causes water eddies, these ribs cause gas eddies that interrupt smooth gas flow, especially at higher gas densities normally found at deeper depths, compounded if the hose diameter is small.

Some manufacturers incorporate specially designed hoses with large-diameter hoses and some even smooth insides while still being as flexible as corrugated hoses.

CCR gas use vs OC gas use

Now that we know a bit more about how open and closed circuit works, we can look at where each comes into play.

As all divers are trained (hopefully ☺), pressure increases with depth, being roughly 1 ata for every 33 ft (10 m) increase in sea water. On open circuit the diver's gas consumption rate increases proportional to the pressure. If a diver were to breathe 0.6 cu ft per minute on the surface, the same diver would use 2.4 cu ft per minute of gas at 100 ft (30 m), and at 330 ft (100 m) the diver would need 6.6 cu ft per minute of gas. An 80 cu ft tank that would have lasted 133 minutes on the surface will now only last 12 minutes at 330 ft (100 m).

The CCR diver, being unaffected by depth can still do 133 minutes at 330 ft (100 m) with the 80 cu ft tank and therefore does not require such a large amount of gas. The CCR diver is then able to complete a dive with far less gas used than the OC diver. Considering the cost of Helium, the savings can be considerable, especially if taking into account that the OC diver will need to carry and use additional tanks to reach the surface and decompress while the CCR diver will just stay on the same two small tanks (diluent and Oxygen) he/she started the dive with.

From the above information it seems that the CCR unit is the clear winner, knocking the OC down with a one-two punch combination (diluent and Oxygen), however, not so fast, as this OC is named Rocky. ☺

OC pros and cons

The first drawback of OC is that it requires large amounts of gas to be carried by the diver to complete deep and long dives. This requires multiple cylinders that need to be analyzed and identified correctly. The diver will be making gas switches underwater as each cylinder is used up.

The risk exists of the diver breathing the incorrect mixture at depth when making a switch. Imagine switching to pure Oxygen at 280 ft, oops. In addition, with every gas change there is a sudden change in mixture percentages, the degree being related to the gas being switched to. The switch is however needed to increase the amount of Oxygen while decreasing the amount of inert gas to accelerate decompression. Even if the diver switches to the correct planned gas, if the gas being switched to was poorly planned the diver is at risk of injury.

Open circuit deep diving is thus very demanding and requires a lot of concentration and discipline. Open circuit is easier to dive in some regards as there is less that can go wrong; however, the CCR diver has more options when things do go wrong.

OC diving gear is normally far cheaper when compared to CCR diving, with new CCR units costing in the range of US $8000 and up. One can easily travel to a diving destination and replace the valve of a large cylinder with an H-valve to provide redundant regulators. Many BCDs are able to attach two cylinders on the back, making independent twins, or one can just attach rigging to side sling the cylinders. This makes OC decompression diving easier when travelling or going to hard to reach places.

CCR pros and cons

Diving with a rebreather requires additional steps when kitting up that an OC diver does not have. The rebreather needs scrubber to extract the CO_2 out of the loop; this material needs to be packed correctly into the unit. The possibility exists for the gas to find a way around the scrubber material if not packed correctly, called breakthrough or channeling. This will cause the CO_2 in the diver's loop to not react with the scrubber material and a buildup of CO_2 will occur. This is one reason why reabreathers are called silent killers, as the symptoms are not always noticed by the diver. However, with correct training and keeping to procedures this is extremely rare and unlikely to happen.

Rebreathers have Oxygen sensors or cells that read the amount of Oxygen in the loop. These sensors normally last from 12 to 18 months and can cost in the range of $40 to about $150 each. Many rebreathers have three Oxygen cells, although some may have four, with only a few having one or two cells. This adds to the maintenance of the rebreather, and the problem that if a cell starts to malfunction a replacement may not always be on hand at your dive destination.

Due to the rebreather keeping a constant partial pressure of Oxygen in the loop, the gas percentage keeps on changing as you change depth. This provides a best gas scenario for any depth the diver is at within his/her dive plan. However, the possibility exists for the Oxygen supply to malfunction, with no Oxygen being added to the loop. If the diver is lax in monitoring his instruments, it is possible for the amount of Oxygen in the loop to reach a point where the diver will black out (most rebreathers have alarms that activate if the level drops below a preset value, normally 0.4 PPO2, with some even injecting O2 automatically if it drops below 0.21 PPO2). On the other hand, the Oxygen solenoid can be stuck open and inject Oxygen into the loop constantly at depth, causing the breathing gas to become toxic. Again, if the diver does not monitor his instruments, injury or death may result.

It should be noted that in training divers are taught to monitor their instruments correctly and handle both above mentioned problems, however the point is that a diver cannot carelessly dive along with a rebreather, even if it is a no decompression dive. Furthermore, note that most rebreathers on the market have visual and audible warnings to alert the driver of a problem.

Due to the rebreather constantly changing the breathing gas to follow a set partial pressure of Oxygen, there is no need to change over or switch to different mixes as the diver ascends. The change is also very smooth as it happens constantly and at the speed of the diver's ascent, compared to OC where the switch happens instantly when the diver changes over and starts breathing a new gas. The rebreather gas change is far easier on the body and allows for optimum off-gassing.

As the diver exhales into the loop, a lot of heat is retained, and on cold diving the diver can be warmer when compared to an OC diver, in addition to having no bubbles (correctly functioning CCR and constant depth) which helps not to scare off marine life and is a great help in caves and wrecks for not dislodging silt from overhead areas as found in OC.

CCR units however require the use and filling of pure Oxygen that is not always available in all locations. An OC diver can still dive and decompress on air or even recreational Nitrox (up to 40%), but without pure Oxygen the rebreather diver cannot use the unit (without using procedures that are not part of normal CCR diving).

Transporting a rebreather unit through customs can sometimes be a problem if they do not normally see diving units, and the scrubber material by itself is a problem to transport, both in appearance and in weight. OC equipment is far easier to transport and many OC divers carry their regulators onto the airplane as hand luggage (although few take their tanks with as it is easier to rent twins).

Gas differences
Using less gas on a CCR unit compared to OC is one of the biggest selling points of rebreathers (apart from ego ☺). Due to the price of Helium, a deep dive can become considerably expensive on OC, especially if you have a high breathing rate.

Thus, one may assume that the rebreather costs far less for the same deep dive, as only a small Tri-Mix and Oxygen cylinder is used. However, many people forget that the rebreather diver still needs bailout tanks with enough gas to bring the diver up from depth including doing all decompression. As the OC diver may have been running a 1.4 PPO2 at depth and the rebreather diver a 1.2 or 1.3 PPO2, the rebreather diver may at the point of bailing out at his/her deepest depth have more decompression obligation than the OC diver and require more ascent and decompression gas than the OC diver.

The bailout tanks need to be calculated as part of the dive cost, including the price for the Oxygen and Tri-Mix diluent cylinder plus the cost of the scrubber. Since the ascent and decompression gas for the CCR diver can be compared to the ascent and decompression gas of the OC diver, the difference in dive cost will be what the OC diver pays for his/her back gas compared to what the rebreather diver pays for scrubber, Oxygen and diluent. Many times the difference is only small.

Only on subsequent dives can the CCR diver start to see some savings. If the diver did not use his/her bailout tanks (some do as an off board diluent, in this case you have to calculate the additional gas you will need by using your bailout else you may not have enough to bail out to when the need arises), then they can be reused for subsequent diving.

With multi day diving and repetitive diving with a rebreather there is no need to constantly refill side sling cylinders after every dive (unless you used it for bailing out). The OC diver however will need to have his back gas and side sling cylinders topped up or refilled.

The rebreather diver will then need to calculate the cost saving that is made per dive trip from using less gas and use that amount to calculate how many dive trips it would take to repay for the unit purchase, additional training, additional shipping cost, and maintenance of the unit. In cases divers may find that the cost saving does not warrant the outlay, especially if dives are not deep and the diver does not do many dives per year.

Conclusion

As can be seen, it is not a case of just going out and purchasing either OC or CCR equipment. There is much consideration and thought that needs to be done.

The first should be the ease of transporting the needed equipment to your intended diving destination, including the ability to fix things in the field. Once you have determined the cost and feasibility of transporting your gear, you need to inquire as to the possibility of obtaining pure Oxygen and scrubber material at your destination, unless you bring your own. If you cannot bring your own scrubber and it will not be available at your destination, there is no point in taking a CCR unit, mostly the case for remote locations.

The next thing will be the cost factor. Oxygen sensors and o-rings in the unit deteriorate regardless of whether or not you use the unit, thus there is a fixed maintenance cost per year and then a running cost. Taking then your yearly cost of maintaining the unit, you divide that amount by the number of dives you will be doing in a year. This will give you a maintenance cost per dive. You can do the same for OC, however it is normally far less on OC.

You can now calculate the cost saving you expect to see by doing repetitive dives on a rebreather. (Remember you still have to pay for the bailout tanks for the first dive.) Taking the gas cost you will save per year, you can divide that saving into the price of purchasing your model of CCR, this will show you how many years of diving you will need to do to break even had you done all the dives on OC. The more dives and deeper dives you do per year, the more the savings on CCR compared to OC and the faster you will break even. Once you have reached your break-even point, you are now actually saving money.

Another point to consider is the skill level needed to dive a rebreather, it is advised that you dive at least one or two dives per month on your unit to stay fresh, if you dive less you start to forget things and it is more dangerous on a CCR unit to be forgetful than on OC.

Divers also need to realize that should the rebreather malfunction on a dive trip then it is often difficult to have it repaired on-site and in cases part or the complete unit will need to be sent back to the manufacturer.

Both OC and CCR have their place with cons and pros for each, know what you get before you buy and you will be a far happier diver.

Chapter 5

Past deep diving experience

Many commercial and military divers enter deep diving or even recreational diving thinking that the skills and methods they learned in military and saturation or commercial diving entitles them to get a certification without doing the actual courses. However, the skills learned in these diving areas may be radically different than recreational diving.

Even when divers have experience in deep saturation diving, those dives most often are done using surface supplied gas and diving chambers. A topside crew is responsible for gas supply and normally calculations of decompression profiles.

In recreational and sports technical diving, the divers most often use either open circuit or a rebreather, carry all or most of their own gas with them, and are responsible for calculating their own decompression profiles. When a problem arises, divers are reliant on their own, and dive buddy's skills as support divers are often not used unless it is a very deep dive. Thus even though a commercial or military diver may have the discipline and mindset to do deep dives, they will need to learn how to use the gear that is used and the methods employed by sports technical divers.

Chapter 6

What route to take

Many divers interested in CCR diving wonder if they should train all the way up to Tri-Mix diver on OC, then cross over to CCR diver, or just go straight into CCR training from the start.

This is a difficult subject and its answer depends on many factors, so let's look at the pros and cons of doing both to help us get a clearer picture of where to go.

If you do not intend to dive deep on OC, it would seem to make sense to go straight to CCR diving all the way to Tri-Mix. Cheaper cost as less gas is used in the training and less time as you do not need to relearn the classes. However, if you did your Tri-Mix on OC, then it is in most cases possible to cross over to Tri-Mix CCR diver with only two to four dives. This will give you the option of diving deep on OC should your rebreather fail or it is impossible to transport the rebreather to your destination. This will give you more freedom in doing deep diving.

Another factor to consider is that, should you have trained deep diving on OC, and you do a dive on CCR and the unit fails, you will be in home territory when you bail out. Although bailing out is part of the drills for CCR divers, many do it once or twice in their training and then never again. With solid OC training you get more experience actually planning and executing deep OC dives, valuable experience for when you need to bail out deep inside a wreck or cave.

Consider also that should you later decide to do deep OC diving but hold only a CCR rating, you will need to start from the bottom as you cannot cross over easily from a Tri-Mix CCR diver to an OC Tri-Mix diver, as is the case for crossing from OC to CCR.

With OC you can easily use a buddy's gear or rent some and do deep dives, however with CCR training it is unit specific and if the unit you rent or borrow is a different rebreather than the one you have trained on, you will not be able to use it until you get trained on it. Note it is not needed to redo all the training up to Tri-Mix for the new unit, once you are CCR Tri-Mix trained you only need to do training on how to use the new unit and you can then dive it to your highest CCR qualification.

If you are travelling to remote places, dive caves or deep wrecks, want flexibility and added experience in doing deep dives, then there is a strong argument for training up to Tri-Mix on OC, then do a crossover to CCR.

Remember, deep down you do not only want the best gear, but also the best experience and knowledge that you can afford.

Chapter 7

Becoming a thinking diver

Many divers find that the longer they have been diving recreationally, the harder it is to transition to technical diving. Recreational divemasters and instructors often find it difficult and get frustrated at the beginning (ego often plays a role for admitting that even though they have been diving for years and are instructors, they do not know everything, and the course is hard for some to do). An open water instructor who just started his Advanced Nitrox diver course once told me *'I have been diving for eight years and know everything there is to know about gas switches.'*

Note, it is not that recreational divers have been doing things wrong, but that they need to understand that the environment and circumstances have changed and so too the way of diving.

The first shock comes as they are suddenly forced to think and come up with creative solutions to problems. Not to say that recreational divers do not think, but many recreational divers book dive trips with resorts or clubs where divemasters or instructors will be leading the dive. All the diver needs to do is follow the dive leader and indicate when he/she reaches a half tank of gas and the dive leader takes care of the rest (navigation and dive speed). If a problem arises the dive leader is normally on hand to help out.

There is nothing wrong with dive leaders leading the dives; in technical diving you can also have a dive leader lead the dive. However, you are required to be more self reliant and will normally need to know when to switch to different mixes without a dive leader telling you to. In most cases you are required to calculate yourself how much gas you are using and when to turn the dive, including how to handle problems like failed dive computers or overrun bottom time as you need to calculate your own decompression obligation. When problems arise you are normally required to handle your own problems, with the dive leader or your buddy only helping when required. A recreational dive guide may think little of finning over to a recreational diver and adding a little air to their BCD, however in technical diving this would raise some eyebrows.

Since going deeper increases the likelihood of gear malfunctioning, in addition to dives not going as planned, the amount of problems that can arise is considerably more than on shallow recreational dives.

Anton Swanepoel

In technical diving, the instructor training you cannot possibly teach you what to do in every circumstance in every environment you will be diving. All the instructor can do is give you a baseline of skills and experiences to use as building blocks and make you a thinking diver so that you can adapt underwater as things happen, using the skills you have been taught (possibly in a different way).

Technical divers normally sit before the dive and think about what can possibly go wrong on the dive and imagine how they would solve the problem, allowing them to be more prepared. This is hardly ever done in recreational diving. The thinking technical diver is then more used to finding solutions for any anticipated problems on the dive. A diver may say, ok what if my main regulator starts to free flow? Followed by a 'no problem', shut the valve down and switch to your secondary regulator as learned.

The thinking technical diver can then combine skills to find new solutions when new problems arise underwater. For instance, divers learn how to remove their gear underwater in addition to switching between back gas and decompression cylinders.

Let's say you are diving in strong current or low visibility and lose contact with your buddy. You proceed to your scheduled decompression stop where you switch to your decompression cylinder, only to find that it is malfunctioning. Now you switch back to your back gas and start your decompression on your back gas. However, you notice that due to the strong current you used more gas than normal and in searching for your buddy you overran your bottom time and do not have enough gas on your back gas to complete the deco obligation.

Here, the thinking diver may decide to remove his gear while breathing off his back gas, then remove one of his regulators (preferably one without a pressure gauge) and replace the regulator on the deco tank with the regulator that was removed from his back gas. The diver can now accelerate the decompression by using the deco tank and still have back gas left should it be needed.

The aim is to make the diver think of new solutions, rather than give up and die. So long as you are alive, possibilities remain to survive. However, give up and you are dead before you breathed your last breath.

The new technical diver might also find that he/she starts to dive differently on recreational dives as well. Things that were taken for granted and done, are now evaluated with 'what if' questions.

Consider a tech diver trained, with redundant buoyancy control devices, regulators, masks, computers, and enough gas to bring two divers to the surface doing a dive to 200 ft, against a novice diver doing a 130 ft air dive on normal recreational gear over a 4000 ft wall. What if the BCD malfunctions, the o-ring on the yoke regulator gives in (or worse, the regulator gives in), the diver loses a fin, or a mask strap breaks. Who is actually the safer diver?

BCD breathing

Taking finding solutions a bit further, imagine you are on a dive in a cave or wreck and either become entangled, lost or have a loss of gas. You are ten minutes away from the exit when you finally come free, find the guideline or close the leak. However, you have only two minutes worth of bottom gas left.

You can use the two minutes of gas to write a lovely poem to your friends and say good-bye, or you can try to swim for the exit and see how far you can get. You may even chance switching to your deco gas and hope not to get an O2 hit. Most people will try to conserve the gas as much as possible by possibly skip breathing and holding their breath. You may possibly double your gas supply to four minutes worth by conserving gas, but you are still short.

There is a different option however, BCD breathing. With BCD breathing you can easily extend your dwindling gas supply by more than three times.

-BCD breathing and diver training

Even though BCD breathing is an option and was looked at in the 1980s by Undercurrent magazine and again in 2011, it is not trained by any recreational or technical agency.

-Death from BCD infection

One reason for not training BCD breathing is the fear of infection from bacteria in the BCD. In 2009, 58-year-old Michael Firth, an active technical diver, became ill and died from breathing aspergillus fumigatus (a micro-organism that exists within all our bodies and in the air, but is usually safely contained by our immune systems). It is unclear why, but Firth apparently took two deep breaths from his wing BCD's manual inflator in testing it, and although he noted that the air tasted moldy he thought no more about it. He later became ill and passed away in December 2009 while awaiting a lung transplant. Later investigation established that the fungus was traced back to the BCD.

-Accidental BCD breathing

Although many trainee divers do not intend it, many actually make mistakes when manually inflating their BCD in the open water class. To inflate the BCD manually one needs to place the manual dump in the mouth, depress the deflator button, and exhale into the BCD. When a breath is exhaled into the BCD, a diver needs to release the dump button and remove the deflator from the mouth to take a fresh breath. However, students often get confused and keep the dump button depressed while holding the deflator in their mouths while taking a breath. What they think is a fresh breath of air is actually the air that is in the BCD bladder. So even though BCD breathing is not taught in classes, it actually happens by accident. Not to mention the many divers that suck the air out of their BCD to allow them to descend faster, especially when descending in a current from a dive boat on drift dives.

-CCR lung breathing

CCR divers breathe from a counter lung that is in effect the same as a BCD wing as it holds air. CCR divers normally disinfect the counter lung after each dive or after a dive trip. However, if the diver becomes lax and does not disinfect the unit completely (including hoses), or the unit has been standing in storage for some time and is not disinfected before use, it is possible that the level of bacteria in the unit could cause lung infection in the diver.

-What is the real risk?

From the reported death and the realization that people do by accident breathe from their BCD, one would wonder how real the risk is. According to David Denning (Professor of Mycology, University of Manchester, UK, and Director of the National Aspergillosis Centre), Firth is the only known death resulting from BCD breathing and it is not known why his body reacted so badly to the infection. Dive medicine Doctor Ian Sibley-Calder also noted that invasive pulmonary aspergillosis is extremely unusual in healthy people with no other history of lung problems or altered immune system.

-Disinfection of your BCD

Since many bacteria can and do enter the BCD, it is a good idea to periodically disinfect the BCD, even if you do not intend to breathe from it. Many dive shops sell commercial disinfectants, however benzalkonium chloride (brand name Zephiran chloride) can also be used, or a 10% bleach solution.

-When the chips are down, roll the dice

So back to our scenario, you can either elect to try to go for the exit and hope you make it, or you can try to extend your gas by BCD breathing. Lung infections are common and normally treatable, drowning is kind of permanent.

-How to BCD breathe in an emergency

There are different ways of doing it, all depending on your depth and exit point. One option is to take a breath from your regulator and then breathe that into your BCD, now inhale and exhale from the BCD up to around three to four times.

Following the third or fourth breath from the BCD, take another fresh breath from your regulator while dumping the gas from the BCD. Exhale again into the BCD and rebreathe as before. Note, if you are not on a solid bottom such as a cave or wreck you may need to add additional air to the BCD from the inflator to regain buoyancy if you dumped too much gas from the wing.

If you are making a short straight ascent then it is possible to continue breathing from the BCD and exhale through your nose when you need to dump some air to slow your ascent. Although highly unlikely that you will ever need it, it is possible to swap gasses by unplugging the BCD inflator from your back gas and connecting it to another tank, just deflate the BCD fully to get the old mix out. Further note that since the O2 content goes down with each breath, your decompression schedule may be incorrect if doing a decompression dive. You can follow missed decompression protocols described in later chapters.

Broken Regulator

If you lost function in all your regulators and your buddy is not present, you can use the same option as BCD breathing to keep you alive while you make your way to the surface. Broken regulators are possible where the nut retaining the lever in the regulator comes undone allowing the level to fall out, disabling the regulator. It has also happened that technicians service a regulator and put the retaining washer the wrong side of the lever, allowing the lever to slip out after a few uses, rendering the regulator useless.

At the very least, if you have a gas supply problem and run into that strange type of diver who does not believe in carrying a spare regulator (octo), you may have an option. In this case it is not needed to rebreathe the BCD gas, you can breathe the tank gas by using the inflator as a regulator. Put the manual inflator mouthpiece in your mouth as if you were going to manually inflate your BCD, and while holding the deflator button fully down press the inflator button gently. Now take a breath as you gently regulate the gas with the inflator button.

Anton Swanepoel

End note

There is always another way or option, do not give up but think of something. Become a survivor not another statistic. No instructor can teach you every trick or skill to cope with every possible scenario that you may face. The best we can do is to make a thinking diver out of you and give you a set of skills and experiences that you can build on and increase. When things go wrong, you then dig into the bag of skills and experiences, you have to find a new solution instead of going, oh crap my instructor did not tell me this could happen.

The same goes for gear configuration, every diver likes his/her gear to be a certain way, some for good reason and others because that is the way they were taught. There is no real right or wrong way, however some setups work better than others in different environments, know the pros and cons for your setup.

Take for instance on a twinset (two tanks), each having its own first stage regulator. You can either run the inflator hoses straight down so that the left post (valve) regulator inflate the main BCD wing and the right post regulator inflate the backup BCD wing while also giving gas to the main regulator. In this instance you will be breathing from a different regulator than what you use to inflate the BCD making breathing and BCD inflation independent. Or you can cross the inflator hoses so that the left post regulator inflate the backup BCD wing and the right post regulator inflates the main BCD wing in addition to giving gas to the main regulator. In this instance the BCD inflation and breathing is not independent as it is coming from the same regulator.

The thought of crossing inflator hoses is that if you are in a cave or ice diving, then you have one fresh clean regulator if your main one malfunctions as this regulator is not used until needed. However, when it does fail you lose breathing and BCD inflation at the same time. This may be OK in a cave, but when are doing wall or deep diving with 4000 ft below you, losing breathing and buoyancy at the same time is not so good. By using one regulator for both BCD inflation and breathing you also do not know if the spare regulator works until you need it.

Another example is slinging all the tanks on one side. The reason normally is from cave diving where you have a battery pack the size of a car battery on one side and cannot clip a stage there. However, if nothing is obstructing putting a tank there, why not place lean mixes on the left and rich mixes on the right? This helps you avoid accidently breathing the wrong mix. Divers sometimes rotate tanks by having the tank they breathe from on the top if having all the tanks on one side, although it works it takes more concentration and work with more potential for errors. Some divers trail tanks behind them, however one needs to realize that you now place a potential breathing gas on only one clip that can break (has happened) in addition to increasing drag.

Be an open-minded diver, if another diver has a setup different than yours, ask why. Sometimes you may just learn a new trick or learn a different way that things are done to where you normally dive. Warm water Caribbean diving is far different from cold-water Jersey diving. Open water and cave or wreck diving is also different and each may require a different setup. By knowing more ways to do things you will become a more flexible diver who can adapt to changing environments. Of course sometimes you do walk away from another diver thinking, dumb ass. But that is technical diving, there are so many ways to do things and many ideas and ways of doing thinks are only personal opinions or theory, including decompression. Find what works for you.

Chapter 8

Effects of deeper diving on the body

The human body is not designed to venture underwater at the extreme pressures found in deeper diving or the time periods spent in the water when doing decompression diving, however it does cope with it reasonably well, or so we think.

There are a number of known changes to the body as we descend underwater, some only seem to be a problem on deep dives, while others occur even on shallow dives. Here are a few.

Bone necrosis

Deep dives, especially deep air dives, have been linked to bone necrosis (dying of parts of bone tissue), called dysbaric osteonecrosis (DON). Although DON is currently not fully understood, it is thought to be due to a complication as a result of ineffective decompression following exposure to high-pressure environments, such as deep diving or tunnel working (compressed gas workers), and comprises necrotic lesions (characteristically multiple and bilateral) in the fatty marrow-containing shafts of the long bones (mostly from the arms and legs), and the ball and socket joints (hips and shoulders); with prevalence of about 17% among compressed air workers and 4.2% among divers.

DON is not unique to humans; cases of DON have even been reported in sperm whales with the severity of symptoms linked to the age of the whale.

-First cases

Although Hippocrates put the concept of DON forward in antiquity, it was not until 1794 before the first modern-day description was written by James Russell of Edinburgh. At this time, infection was thought to be the main culprit. However, in 1888 necrosis of the femoral head without infection was noted by Konig (aseptic necrosis). Radiological confirmation of aseptic bone necrosis in compressed air workers was reported by Bornstein and Plate in 1911 and Bassoe in 1913, with the first report of aseptic bone necrosis in a diver being reported in 1936. Currently, many air decompression tables used for tunnel workers seem to be inadequate to prevent DON. Some countries such as Germany have put Oxygen decompression in regular use (from 1972), however some countries still do not allow regular Oxygen decompression for tunnel workers due to the fire risk of using Oxygen in tunnels.

-Causes

There are a few theories as to what leads to the bone death, with Nitrogen taking the largest blame.

-Nitrogen

The leading thought currently is that Nitrogen embolism (Nitrogen bubbles forming out of solution) blocks the supply of Oxygen and nutrients to the bone, however it has been shown that certain blood cells become more rigid at pressures above 4 ata and may then not be able to pass through capillary walls, obstructing blood flow in the capillaries. It is also thought that pieces of fat from damaged tissue and blood platelet clumps that may form in the presence of inert gas bubble contribute to the blood blockage.

Since the long bones of the arms and legs are rich in very fatty white bone marrow that can hold a considerable amount of gas, it is thought that the gas coming out of the bones on decompression may form bubbles. Due to the bubbles forming directly outside the bone, it may then block blood flow to the bone.

-Oxygen

Oxygen toxicity is seen as another possible contributor to bone necrosis. Although it is known that higher partial pressures of Oxygen cause blood vessels to constrict and limit the amount of Oxygen reaching tissues, it is suggested that small blood vessels to the bones may constrict so much that it limits blood flow below an adequate level to the bone tissue, resulting in bone death.

High pressures of Oxygen also modify collagen tissue (a group of naturally occurring proteins), interfering with circulation and nutrition to the bone. Bones are life cells that are connected by collagen tissue. The high pressure of Oxygen also causes fat cells to swell, raising the internal pressure in the bone and possibly cutting off blood supply by constricting blood vessels.

-Pressure

Another contributor is thought to be the pressure itself of the dive. Fluid transmits pressure evenly. At depth the pressure is transferred evenly to all the tissues with even muscle behaving fluid like. However, the bones are the only rigid tissue in the body and temporary pressure differences may cause damage to the bones. This may explain why the rate of descent has been linked to increased DON occurrences and that DON seems to be unrelated to DCS, occurring with or without DSC.

-DCS

Due to bubble formation being linked to decompression not done correctly, it follows that proper decompression schedules must be followed. However, dysbaric osteonecrosis is rarely found in divers doing dives on air shallower than 165 ft, especially if divers follow correct decompression procedures.

It is thought that dysbaric osteonecrosis is a possible delayed reaction to decompression sickness and decompression stress, with silent bubbles forming at depth being a big cause as symptoms may not be seen or felt or may only cause extreme tiredness without pain.

Predisposition to dysbaric osteonecrosis includes the following:
years of diving history, doing long dives - two or more hours, diving deeper than 100 ft – especially deeper than 165 ft on air, DCS history - especially if residual symptoms remain, being overweight, and a fast rate of compression (rapid descent).

-Early detection

The suggestion is that an MRI scan for DON should be done after a decompression incident, especially if osteoarthromuscular pain occurs. The MRI can screen for osteomedullar damage that may worsen if diving is continued where it could change to bone necrosis. The damaged areas show up as altered bone density.

-Osteonecrosis on divemasters and dive instructors

A study done on 58 divers working as divemasters or instructors with at least 500 dives that had never performed industrial and commercial dives, and did not have a diagnosis of osteonecrosis, had the following findings. 25% of the divers had DON lesions, indicating a very high DON prevalence when considering they had thorough dive training and strictly practiced decompression rules. It is believed that the high prevalence is a result of frequent and sometimes deep dives for many years. It is suggested that divemasters and instructors be kept under periodic screening for DON lesions as is the case with professional commercial divers in order to help reduce morbidity from DON. Bone necrosis has in some cases only shown up months and even years after a single exposure, often with no other indication of hyperbaric stress.

-Vacuum phenomena

Vacuum phenomena (bubbles forming due to vacuum as joints move) are seen in bone necrosis and raises the question if viscous adhesion in joint movement can generate enough force to separate the articular cartilage from bone, and if exposure to increased inert gas pressure raises the risk of it occurring.

-Factors that can pre-dispose you to bone necrosis

The following is seen to possibly pre-dispose a person to bone necrosis; diabetes, hyperadrenocorticism (Cushing's syndrome; a hormone disorder caused by high levels of cortisol in the blood), radiotherapy, alcoholism, and arterial sclerosis (hardening of the arteries). Smoking reduces bone density and can predispose or aggravate existing bone damage.

-Silent bubbles and necrosis

It is thought that intravascular gas bubbles that are asymptomatic may have hidden effects such as aseptic necrosis and changes in the blood-brain barrier perfusion (altered blood flow to the brain).

-Common sites for necrosis

Walder did a study on 281 compressed air workers in 1969 and found that lesions were mostly seen in the lower thigh at the knee (40%), followed by the shoulder (29%), the hip (16%), and lastly the knee below the knee cap (15%). However, necrosis can occur in any bone in the body.

-Bone marrow necrosis

Bone marrow necrosis is invariably present with bone necrosis and is thought to possibly be the primary event, later confirmed in tests by Walder and Stothard (1978). It is thought that clusters of fat cells in the marrow lie in compartments (made up of bone trabeculae) which swell up due to gas released during decompression, restricting their blood supply that can cause cell death. However, in studies it was found that it is the partial pressure of Oxygen that affects cell size increase more than the total ambient pressure.

-Treatment

Although it does occur that improvement is seen without treatment and that some lesions do not grow as large as to cause bone collapse, often the only treatment is bone or joint replacement when core decompression, bone grafting and electrical stimulation fails. However, treatment is not always successful and it is best treated by prevention by following correct decompression procedures. It is advised that all DCS symptoms should be treated with HBO treatment due to the high relationship with necrosis and DCS incidents.

-Conclusion

Due to the higher rate of DON in commercial, sports and recreational divers than military divers it is thought that following correct decompression schedules helps prevent DON, and that DON is not a factor of deep diving but rather incorrect decompression practices; since military divers follow stricter selection criteria, decompression schemes and medical surveillance than commercial, recreational and sports divers.

Hearing loss

The human ear has a frequency range from about 20 Hz to 20 kHz with a dynamic range in excess of 100 dB although it is most sensitive in the 1 and 6 kHz range with maximum sensitivity at around 4 kHz.

It is known that divers need to equalize their ears as they descend, yet many people abuse their ears and do not equalize correctly. Hearing loss is found in divers due to the constant pressure change and acute barotrauma. Divers may even become deaf if rupturing an eardrum. In commercial diving, the noise of gas flowing into hyperbaric chambers, gas circulating in the helmet, and noise of working underwater may contribute to hearing loss.

Technical divers often have short available bottom times for deep dives, especially when doing dives on open circuit. Divers often swim hard and fast to get to the bottom, as time lost on descent is bottom time lost. On rapid descents divers often do not equalize their ears fast enough and barotrauma may occur.

Noise from regulator bubbles are also thought to play a role in long term hearing loss, especially if the bubbles are directed directly past the diver's ear. Hearing underwater is less sensitive if the diver's ear is immersed (possibly due to the tympanic membrane movement being dampened by the water), thus when helmet diving the noise from bubbles is even more pronounced.

Breathing gases other than air may also affect a diver's hearing. Due to the ears containing gas-filled cavities, any changes in pressure and gas density could be expected to affect hearing, either transiently or long-term. To test for hearing loss in divers, a study was done by Molvaer and Albrektsen and also by Talmi on divers and non divers of similar ages. The results from both tests showed a greater hearing loss in both studies for divers compared to non divers. In another study by Molvaer it was found that divers were more hearing impaired over all frequencies, divers' hearing deteriorated faster compared to non-divers, high-frequency hearing is lost first, and that smoking potentiates high-frequency hearing loss.

Ear infection and barotrauma play a large part in hearing loss in divers, together with noisy boat engines and the high pitched noise from gas entering a decompression chamber, as well as the noise of underwater tools. Many recreational professional divers also forget the damage done to their ears when filling tanks. The noise of a compressor and the sudden high pitched sound when fill lines are drained causes damage to the ears, so too draining tanks in order to change the blend. To limit the noise, place a towel over the valves when draining tanks or fill lines to save your hearing. Blowing your dust cap dry with your tank creates noise that can affect your hearing, not to mention being annoying, rather use a towel or T-shirt.

Blood changes

It has been noted by Pimlott, Ormsby and Cross that white blood cell deformability and filterability decreased by 81% after a four hour exposure to air at 1.5 bar. It is not known if the ambient pressure or the elevated pressures of O2 is the cause.

Compression Arthralgia

Compression Arthralgia, also called 'Compression Pains', results from increases in external pressure surrounding the body. Any diver may experience it and the pain is mostly experienced in the knees, shoulders, fingers, back, hips, neck, and ribs, with occasionally severe lower back pain, often described as deep aching pain (similar to Type I DCS). The pain may be sudden in onset and intense at first then lessening over time. A dry gritty feeling may also be felt within joints.

Compression Arthralgia is related to depth and rate of compression with symptoms usually seen at around 200 ft (60 m) and increasing with depth. Symptoms may be aggravated by exercise and individual susceptibility.

Although symptoms are normally seen in saturation diving, they may occur at around 100 ft (30 m) with rapid compression rates (normally air diving) in sports divers. On dives using Helium in the breathing mix and slow compression rates, symptoms are normally only seen around 300 ft (91 m); however, below 600 ft (182 m) symptoms may occur even with very slow decompression rates.

Symptoms can be from mild irritating pain to crippling, limiting activity, and even further excursion. Symptoms normally lessen over time at depth, however the pain may persist even in the decompression part of the dive until the diver has reached shallower depths. The pain is distinguishable from DCS in that it started on the descent or bottom portion of the dive before decompression was started, and that the symptoms decreases with ascent.

-Causes

The complete mechanics is currently not known, however the current thought is that due to the sudden increase in tissue gas tension surrounding the joints, a gas induced osmosis is produced that in turn produces cavitation due to an imbalance between the inert gas in the blood and that in the synovial fluid and articular cartilage. Water then shifts from the joint to the higher osmolarity blood, interfering with joint lubrication that in turn causes the pain.

-Treatment

Since this is pressure induced, symptoms normally disappear as the diver returns to the surface. Provided there was no joint damage due to activities, there is no long-term effect and no treatment needed. However, if damage has occurred due to activity or load bearing while the joints had no proper lubrication, then pain might be felt when returning to the surface. This pain can be confused for DCS, however recompression would relieve DCS pain. Further examination of the joints would be needed to determine the degree of damage and treatment needed for recovery.

Adaption to DCS

It has been noted from studies that nuclei are shrunk in size and eliminated due to compression. It takes around a week for the nuclei to regenerate, this is called the adaption period. Thus with frequent diving the number of nuclei is seen to be reduced and a reduction in DCS has been observed. Although other factors have to be added, frequent exposure to pressure (deep diving) can reduce the risk of DCS for that dive profile, however as depth is increased beyond the adaption depth, DCS risk will return to normal.

Lung volume changes

A study done by Thorsem found that divers do not have larger vital capacities compared to non divers, and in fact may have reduced vital capacities, being consistent with small airway dysfunction and with the transient changes seen in lung function after a saturation dive.

The study suggests that there are cumulative long-term effects of diving on lung functions, and a study by Lehnigk indicates that divers develop some degree of airflow obstruction due to airway narrowing. Although pulmonary diffusion capacity deteriorates with age, this process may be accelerated in divers.

A study made by Dr J W Reed of the Department of Physiological Sciences, University of Newcastle, on offshore deep saturation divers, found acute lung volume changes after a deep dive. (Reduction of 5 to 7% in maximum flow volume and 5% reduction in gas exchange capacity.)

The loss in lung function did recover over time (time was dependent on the depth of the dive and the decompression done, although dive time played a larger role). If a second decompression dive was done before lung function returned to normal it could affect on and off-gassing, including possible long-term damage as noted from other tests.

The Diving Medical Advisory Committee argued that damage done to the lungs should take the same time to heal as it takes to occur, thus it was suggested that repetitive dives need a surface interval at least as long as the previous dive's total dive time, which was implemented as required practice for UK operations. It was also found in studies that lung tissue gets over extended (hyperinflated) and can predispose the diver to possible lung injuries.

A follow up study by Mrs M E Simpson for the UK Health division on offshore workers showed that lung function and volume reduction occur in both air and saturation dives and is thought to be from hyperoxia, VGE and the work of breathing at depth (work of breathing at 330 ft (100 m) is five times more than on the surface). In some cases, lung function remained reduced for months after a deep dive. Evidence showed that the damage is cumulative and in cases long term.

-Short term lung volume changes
On descent, the gas in the intestines is compressed which results in a lowering of the diaphragm and an increase in vital capacity. A 6.5% increase in vital capacity has been noted by Schilling and coworkers, and Zannini and coworkers reported an average of 13% increase at 100 ft (30 m) with a lowering of about 2.3 cm of the diaphragm. Note that the heart shifts as the diaphragm lowers. The diaphragm slowly returns to normal as gas enters the abdominal space (intestines) due to gas swallowing and fermentation. If the time at depth was sufficient to allow the intestines to expand to normal or near normal size, on ascent the intestines can expand and compress the diaphragm upwards, lowering vital capacity. This is possibly why a reduction in vital capacity has been noted in saturation divers on decompression.

The compression of the intestines also results in a suction in the large splanchnic area that results in vasodepletion in other body areas that results in increased heart rate (note, heart rate is reduced with high inspired PO2), increased stroke volume, and constriction in the small peripheral arteries (reducing blood to peripherals).

Breathing resistance due to depth

Due to gasses becoming denser as the depth increases, breathing resistance will increase to move the denser gas. However, since a larger volume of gas is moved in each breath, turbulence increases significantly and has an increased effect on breathing resistance. Breathing rate should be slowed down to reduce turbulence and breathing resistance (slow deep breaths). Note that faster breathing also does not give the lungs enough time to exchange CO_2 from the blood and take up O_2, resulting in CO_2 build up and O_2 starvation, triggering faster breathing. This can result in increased gas consumption or over breathing of equipment (trying to breathe more volume of gas than a regulator can supply) that may lead to CO_2 poisoning and possibly panic.

However, it should be noted that CO_2 being about 20 times more soluble than O_2 may have enough time to clear the lungs on fast breathing while O_2 may not have enough time to enter, creating an O_2 deficit without an increase in CO_2. It should also be noted that CO_2 is first released in the breathing cycle as O_2 uptake occurs faster when the hemoglobin has released CO_2 and blood pH level returned to normal, thus O_2 uptake is fastest in the last part of each breath cycle. This is the reason for rapid breathing after hard exercise, not to get more O_2 in the system, but to get the CO_2 out as fast as possible, at the cost of air consumption since air consumption matters little on the surface.

Exostosis

Exostosis (also known as surfer's ear) are hard, bony growths in the ear canal that can trap dirt and wax and even grow so big that they can completely block the ear canal. Exostosis is believed to be the body's defense against repeated contact with cold water in the ears. Although this is normally found with cold water divers, it can happen to warmer climate divers as well. The colder the water and the longer the diver remains in the water (main problem for cold water technical divers with long deco), the bigger the problem.

Exostosis is also seen with other activities in cold, wet, windy conditions such as kayaking, sailing, jet skiing and surfing. The best way to prevent this from happening is to wear a neoprene hood or diving earplugs such as *Doc's Pro Plugs,* as they keep a warm pocket of air in the canal, blocking cold water and air out without loss of hearing and balance, see www.proplugs.com

Treatment for exostosis normally means drilling the ear canal open while the patient is under general anesthesia, however new techniques are being used where a 1 mm chisel is used to chisel pieces of the bone off while the patient is under local anesthesia. For more information on exostosis see 'Ear Pain'
www.antonswanepoelbooks.com/ear_pain.php

Neurological Effects

From studies done on divers, statistically significant deviations and dysfunction from normal was found in cognition, memory and spinal cord functions. Most were from saturation divers or divers suffering from severe neurological decompression sickness. Todnem found in a study of neurologic examinations on 40 air and saturation divers and 100 controls that the divers had significantly more general nervous system complaints and more abnormal neurologic findings than the controls. Most symptoms were difficulties in concentration and problems with long- and short-term memory.

A study by Peters, Levin, and Kelly on divers with CNS (central nervous system) DCS found unequivocal neurologic deficits implicating multiple supraspinal lesions. The suggestion is that multiple CNS lesions occur secondary to decompression illness.

Research made by Palmer, Calder, and Hughes suggests significant damage occurs at a subclinical level in decompression illness cases, while a report by Morild and Mork showed ependymal damage in the brain. Ependymal cells line all the brain cavities and control the production and flow of cerebrospinal fluid. If this process is disrupted it affects the brain broadly with dysfunctions of motor, sensory, memory, and cognitive functions. From the studies it was found that the largest loss of ependymal cells was found in professional divers without saturation experience.

Studies done at the University of Wisconsin-Madison on no decompression dive profiles using sheep, found that short deep air dives produced a significantly higher percentage (68% compared to 10%) CNS DCS than long shallow dives, with the long shallow dives producing more limb bends and transient chokes. The total number of DCS hits was the same for either short deep or long shallow dives with the model used.

The London Hyperbaric Medical Service and the Underwater Centre Fort William did tests (September 1985 to December 1986) on professional divers (218 divers no DCS history, 64 divers DCS history, and 61 trainee commercial divers) and found that short- and long-term memory and reasoning skills were significantly affected compared to new trainee divers. They also noted that divers that had a history of DCS significantly fared worse in performance than their colleagues with no DCS history. Thus, it was shown that memory and reasoning ability loss was linked to the number of years diving and greatly affected for those with a DCS history.

Personality Changes

In 1959 Rozsahegyi reported changes in caisson workers that suffered from DCS. It was found that men that suffered from CNS DCS and were previously calm and reserved were easily provoked to go into rages and also impulsive, five years after the DCS incident. Pathological drunkenness, alcohol intolerance, dizziness and headaches were also noted. Although these symptoms were a result of CNS DCS, they can occur without DCS, and Rozsahegyi suggested it may be from repeated decompression.

From studies on tunnel workers who never had DCS it was found that personality changes did occur in some of the workers over time, and that these changes may be due to the effects of silent bubbles that do not cause clinical DCS.

Neuropsychometric Changes

A study by Edmonds showed that abalone divers develop a syndrome of reduced intellectual capacity. Studies suggested an impairment of cognitive function in divers who have experienced decompression sickness, with possible impairment of memory and verbal reasoning. However, a study done on 43 Royal Netherlands Navy mine-clearance divers with at least 15 years of military diving experience with a range from 734 to 2800 dives showed no evidence of neuropsychometric deficits due to extensive diving exposure. This contrasts with some tests made in deep saturation divers where brain lesions and neuropsychometric deficits were detected. Due to the use of conservative decompression procedures by the Navy divers it is concluded that neuropsychometric deficits can be prevented by following correct and conservative diving protocols and procedures.

A study using magnetic resonance imaging (MRI) on a cohort of German divers who regularly undertook deep, repetitive dives found evidence of permanent cerebral lesions and in some, evidence of damage to the cervical vertebral discs.

A study was done by German researchers using cranial MRI on 88 divers who regularly do deep dives and had around 600 to 800 dives logged. The study discovered that 12 divers had brain lesions and that five of those divers had a PFO. It is believed that PFO and ASD contribute significantly to unexplained incidences of DCS.

In a study done on deep divers by Vaernes in 1983 at the Norwegian Underwater Technology Centre, some short- and long-term psychological changes were noted after the dive compared to tests done before a deep dive (experimental deep dives, some ranging to 686 m). Divers showed reduced hand grip strength, impaired memory, and reduced cognitive abilities that only returned to normal after a year in some divers. Inactiveness, attention problems and depression were noted in divers and lasted up to six months, leading one diver to seek psychological help.

After the 1981 Atlantis 3 dive to 686 m, one diver reported memory loss and concentration problems with feelings of sadness and anxiety. The diver was an experienced commercial diver with over 2000 dives. The same symptoms were noted in a team of six divers after a dive to 549 m where they suffered memory problems (such as not remembering where they left their car keys or paychecks), this lasted for several months. (All six divers were tested three years later and found that all symptoms disappeared.)

Encephalomyelopathy

In a report published by Hallenbeck in 1978 it shows a correlation between the development of encephalomyelopathy (Leigh's disease) and repeated decompression. Encephalomyelopathy causes mutations in the mtDNA (mitochondria DNA) that can cause mitochondria to fail or to function improperly, that in turn causes a chronic lack of energy, affecting the central nervous system and inhibiting motor functions and in some cases resulting in death.

Systemic Effects

Ocular changes were found in divers from studies done by investigators such as Polkinhorne, Scholz, Day, Kania and Holden. Doran documented alterations in liver enzymes, while heart effects were found by Maehle and Stuhr, and skin effects by Ahl'en, Iverson, Risberg, Volden, Aarstet and associates.

Considerable attention has been given to how the eyes are affected due to diving. In a study by Polking of the ocular in 84 divers, significantly more abnormalities of the retinal pigment epithelium were found compared to a group of non-divers. The number of occurrences of fundus abnormality found related to the length of diving done by the diver. Many of the changes in the eye were consistent with blockage of retinal and choroidal vessels, either from bubbles during decompression or altered behavior of blood constituents during conditions of increased pressure.

Sholz however found no changes or retinal damage that affects color vision in divers. Recent examination and study on microvessal damage of diver's retinas has shown that the eye may be a primary site of bubble formation on ascent. Studies on offshore workers showed lesions in the eyes of divers, even for those not doing saturation diving.

Due to the eye being connected to the brain, it is affected in the same manner as the brain with CNS DCS. Tests have revealed lesions in the eyes of divers the same as in the brain.

A study done by Day on pupil cycle time of divers had equivocal findings, and a study done by Kania on professional divers who never had DCS had fundal changes similar to divers who had had fundal disease. These tests show that diving may cause permanent degenerative changes in the fundus of the eye, although a study done by Holden on 26 divers who had practiced safe diving for 10 years showed no significant changes against the control group. Thus, eye damage and macular abnormalities found in the eyes of divers can be prevented and controlled by safe diving.

A study done by Doran found that significant alterations to liver enzymes were present in saturation divers, and a study done by Stuhr and Maehle on rats found that repeated exposure to increased pressures resulted in a reduced cardiac function, mass and morphology.

Diver's hand

Diver's hand is a common skin disorder among saturation divers, however it can occur to any diver that spends long hours in the water and seems to be caused by generation of clefts in the upper two thirds of the stratum curium.

With no inflammation or infection detected in divers it is suspected that physical or chemical factors may be the cause. Since up to 50% of divers with diver's hand showed symptoms in the saturation part of the dive, decompression itself is seen as having little or no relevance for development of diver's hand.

Diver's hand is extensive skin peeling of the upper skin layers of both the palms of the hands and occasionally of the soles of the feet, and there is no effective protection or treatment available. Symptoms of diver's hand are redness or whiteness of the skin, itchiness, dryness with cracking and peeling of skin, tightness and stiffness of the skin making movement difficult, swelling of hands or feet, scaling, peeling, soreness, and pins and needles.

The symptoms appeared at any time before or after decompression, and from studies done in 1990, 1994 and 1995 it was reported that 83% of saturation divers have experienced diver's hand at some time in their career. The symptoms normally last for one to two weeks, however in some cases symptoms have been reported to last up to six weeks.

Treatment for diver's hand is mostly treating the symptoms (dry skin). Hand cream and time out of the water seem to be the best treatment.

Cellular Changes

A study of cell changes was done by Fox. 77 air divers and 76 Heliox divers were compared to two control groups, 75 oil rig workers and 52 non oil-rig workers. 3.9% of the divers had an unusually high number of structural aberrations in a small portion of the dividing lymphocytes. The defects and damage were so extreme that the cells are likely to die during mitosis. None of the controls had similar damage.

Immersion in cold water

Although cold water diving is not only found at deeper depths, diving deep often results in passing through thermo clines and entering colder water layers. In addition, deep diving often results in longer dive times that can chill the diver over time if the correct exposure equipment is not worn.

When the body is immersed in cold water, blood is shifted to the core of the body and the central blood volume increases by about 700 ml. The heart has to work harder as cardiac output increases by 30% while systemic vascular resistance (SVR) decreases by 30% (SVR refers to the resistance to blood flow offered by all the systemic vasculature, excluding the pulmonary vasculature (lungs)). Tissue perfusion increases with no rise in Oxygen consumption and plasma volume increases as fluids move from the tissues to the vascular space (normally within the first 30 minutes), this leads to diuresis (increased excretion of urine), natriuresis (the process of excretion of sodium in the urine), and kaliuresis (the process of excreting potassium in the urine) after about ½ hour to 2 hours of immersion.

If the temperature is below a critical level, the body will try to conserve heat by vasoconstriction (narrowing of the arteries) in the peripheral body parts and limiting blood flow to around 10-15ml/minute/100g tissue. If shivering occurs to try to build body heat, then Oxygen consumption increases, which can in turn raise respiration rate.

Anton Swanepoel

Vasoconstriction and blood redistribution does not always affect inert gas division rates, however staying still in cold water will greatly reduce whole-body inert gas exchange, while exercising in cold water will increase whole body inert gas exchange.

Any increase in blood flow (such as light exercise) greatly increases inert gas elimination and reduces DCS risk while reducing decompression time. However, this is only true if no bubbles are present, as exercise greatly increases the risk of DCS when bubbles are present. Also note that from tests it seems that light to mild continuous exercise does not increase bubble formation, where heavy or intermittent exercise does.

Interestingly, while it is known that cardiac output increases due to immersion in water (thus diffusion may increase especially to fatty tissue as their blood flow is related to arterial pressure), but a head-down tilt position also increases cardiac output (fast drops to the bottom with a head-down position stresses the heart immensely).

Interestingly, when the body is immersed in 35 $^{\circ}$C water as opposed to 37 $^{\circ}$C water, there was a reduction in vital capacity of around 5-6% due to blood flow into the thorax. Immersion in 20 $^{\circ}$C water caused a drop in vital capacity of around 12%. In tests the blood flow to the thorax was hindered by applying tourniquets to the arms and legs, when the tourniquets were released vital capacity dropped. Although inert gas elimination is not affected much by vital capacity, it is interesting to note how the body reacts to cold exposure.

Although many divers will wear a drysuit in cold water and not be affected that much by the cold, it should still be noted that a drysuit can fail and flood. In this case, the diver will immediately be chilled by the cold water rushing in. The chilling will affect decompression times, if the diver survives the cold. It has been shown from tests on immersion of oilrig divers with a life vest and immersion suit that survival beyond ½ hour in cold water is very optimistic.

-Hormones causing vasodilation and vasoconstriction
Systemic hormones such as angiotensin (a decapeptide hormone that is formed from the plasma glycoprotein angiotensinogen) and vasopressin (a hormone secreted by cells of the hypothalamic nuclei and stored in the posterior pituitary) cause vasoconstriction and affect gas diffusion.

Kinins, a group of vasoactive straight-chain polypeptides that is formed by kallikrein-catalyzed cleavage of kininogens causes vasodilation in addition to altering vascular permeability. Histamine, amine, C5H9N3 that is produced by decarboxylation of histidine and serotonin (5-hydroxytryptamine (5-HT) a hormone and neurotransmitter) cause vasodilation.

-Cold water adaption

It has been found that repeated cold water exposure alters the metabolic and cardiovascular response to cold water. Thus over time the vasoconstriction to limbs due to immersion of cold water lessens. As blood flow is then not affected as much as when vasoconstriction occurs, it may lessen the risk of DCS. Thus a diver constantly diving in cold water may be less at risk than a warm water diver making a dive in cold water. The result may be seen in alacaluf and aborigines that can tolerate a large decrease in skin temperature without an increase in metabolic rate, shivering or vasoconstriction. For interest, 96.8 °F (36 °C) water temperature is where maximum vasodilatation occurs, and 50 °F (10 °C) is where maximum vasoconstriction occurs.

Hyperoxia-induced myopia

Hyperoxia-induced myopia is damage to the lens in the eye making the lens less flexible resulting in the inability to focus, thus vision is impaired, and is a result of prolonged exposure to elevated Oxygen partial pressures, normally from multiple consecutive days of diving (especially long CCR dives). By reducing the Oxygen partial pressure and exposure length, the symptoms can be reduced or avoided. Symptoms may take weeks or months to clear up, however in some cases permanent damage may occur.

Nitrogen narcosis

Rapture of the deep. In diving, Nitrogen causes narcosis and is thought to play a major role in decompression sickness. Nitrogen narcosis is normally only noted at depths greater than 100 ft, but has been seen in people at shallower depths. The first record about Nitrogen narcosis was by Junod in 1835 when he noted that breathing compressed air affected the brain functions and mood of the person. In 1861 Green reported a feeling of sleepiness, hallucinations and impaired judgment, and later reports on tunnel workers showed impairment and loss of consciousness at 100 m (330 ft) on air. It was not until 1935 however that Behnke found Nitrogen to be the cause of the narcosis.

When diving beyond 130 ft it is seen as outside recreational diving. Training for deep air diving up to 180 ft in technical diving exists; two agencies that offer this training are IANTD and TDI.

The deepest depth accepted when diving on air is normally 218 ft due to the Oxygen in the air reaching 1.6 PPO2 at this depth. Although many people have gone deeper on air, it is not recommended due to the extreme narcosis, O2 toxicity and the possibility of deep water blackout.

The general thought is that Nitrogen narcosis is caused by the Nitrogen gas dissolving into the lipid bi-layer of cell membranes causing the cell to expand, which at elevated pressures interferes with the neurotransmitter receptors and protein mechanisms of the cells (mostly spinal column and brain cells). The enlarged cells seem to cause short circuiting of signals sent between the brain and the rest of the body. A signal sent to your hand to press the power inflator button to stop your descent may reach your left little toe, confusing it like a chameleon in an M&M packet, not only has he got all the colors but he is sweet as well. ☺

Another thought is that of reduced surface tensions. Transmission of impulses through synapses occurs due to depolarization and repolarization of the pre-synaptic and post-synaptic membrane. The lining (being lipoprotein) is penetrated by pores that allow sodium to pass. Gasses when at narcotic pressures cause the surface tension of the lipoprotein to water interface to decrease by around 0.39 dyne/cm that interferes with sodium passage through the pores, resulting in interference with cell signals. However, neither theory has been totally proven nor disproved, and both may be correct.

It takes only one to two minutes for the ambient pressure in the brain to reach that of the pressure in the lungs. This will produce a small delay in narcosis if one descends very quickly and is the main reason for that feeling of someone closing the door on you when doing rapid descents. Rapid descents can potentiate Nitrogen narcosis due to CO2 retention, especially if the diver did a hard swim before descending without a rest to clear out the excess CO2 that was built up in the swim.

-Nitrogen narcosis signs

0 to 33 ft There is almost no symptoms to detect.

33 to 100 ft One might have mild impairment of thought and reasoning, and a mild feeling of euphoria.

100 to 165 ft Motor skills are more affected and the ability to do calculations and make decisions is impaired. The effect of fixating on one idea is present, like only watching your depth gauge. The diver might experience a sense of well being and could become over confident in his/her diving abilities leading to major risk-taking decisions, or the diver may experience the flip side to this and the feeling of impending doom and panic may overwhelm the diver.

165 to 230 ft A diver can become sleepy and judgment is heavily impaired. Simple motor skills are severely affected and delayed reactions are noted, making it difficult for the diver to focus on the dive plan, gas consumption, time, depth, and coming back. Insensitivity to body signals such as being cold may occur that could lead to hypothermia without the diver knowing he/she is cold. The breathing may slow down that saves gas and many divers are amazed at how low their breathing rate is on deep air dives; however this can lead to CO_2 build up and CO_2 poisoning. Hallucinations, hysteria and dizziness may occur and if the diver does not ascend at this point he/she may not come back.

230 to 300 ft Loss of memory and mental confusion occur in most divers, and dexterity and judgment are heavily affected. The diver has extreme difficulty concentrating on keeping track of multiple tasks and normally only fixates on one, such as depth, forgetting gas supply and dive time. It takes great concentration and mental focus to follow multiple tasks at this depth at one time.

300 to 500 ft Heavy hallucinations and dizziness occur, with a very strong sense of impending doom and impending blackout. The diver can lose the sense of time and space and not know where they are. Unconsciousness and death are a very strong possibility in most divers. Even if the diver ascends at this point narcosis will still affect them for some time and the diver may blackout on the way up.

500 ft and below The possibility for blackout is extreme and almost certain in most divers. Dan Manion holds the record at 509 ft (155 m) on air set in 1994. Successful dives by others deeper than 400 ft on air are documented, however more deaths have occurred than successes and one death is one too many. Due to the availability of Tri-Mix, doing deep air diving below 220 ft is highly discouraged and very rarely done these days.

Nitrogen narcosis varies from diver to diver and from dive to dive. You do not build up a tolerance to Nitrogen narcosis; your body just becomes accustomed to operating in a state of narcosis and mostly operates by muscle memory (doing a skill repeatedly). Thus, any poorly learned skills will be hard to remember, and complicated dive plans will be difficult to follow or remember. Diving habits good or bad will automatically be done and can either save or kill you. Slowing down your actions and staying calm will help you in completing tasks easier while under narcosis.

There are several things that can elevate the effects of the Nitrogen narcosis you will experience. These include but are not limited to, the speed of your descent, excess CO_2 left in the body before descending, CO_2 build up (skip breathing or natural CO_2 retention), mental state of the diver, certain drugs, caffeine, stress, alcohol, fatigue, hard work underwater (swimming hard against a current), negative attitude, and diving outside your knowledge, training and comfort zone. Note that some motion sickness medication can cause sedation, loss of judgment, and aggravation of Nitrogen narcosis.

It should be noted that to discourage deep air record attempts, the Guinness World Records ceased to publish records on deep air dives. The current recorded records are:

1947 Frédéric Dumas, 307 ft (94 m)
1959 Ennie Falco, 435 ft (133 m) (not verified)
1965 Tom Mount and Frank Martz, 360 ft (110 m)
1967 Hal Watts and AJ Muns, 390 ft (120 m)
1968 Neil Watson and John Gruener, 437 ft (133 m)
1990 Bret Gilliam, 452 ft (138 m) (Gilliam remained functional at depth, being able to complete maths problems and answer questions written on a slate beforehand).
1993 Bret Gilliam, 475 ft (145 m), again reporting mostly not being affected by Nitrogen narcosis or Oxygen toxicity.
1994 Dan Manion, 509 ft (155 m), (current record) (Manion reported being almost completely incapacitated by narcosis).

-How narced are you?

A study to determine if people can tell when their performance is being affected by Nitrogen narcosis was done by the Diving Diseases Research Centre for the Health and Safety Executive (2004). It was found that in general divers knew they were affected, but were unable to correctly determine the degree by which they were affected. Divers may think that their response times are fast and without errors, however the reality is not always the case.

Experienced divers often believe that due to their experience they are not affected much if at all by narcosis and can function normally at depth even when they are in fact suffering from narcosis (sometimes referred to as "adaptation").

-Is it all in the mind?

A study was done where divers were told to expect narcosis at different depths 33 ft to 82.5 ft (10 m or 25 m). The divers did exactly that, they expected narcosis at the depths given to them and reported being narced at those depths. This gives some weight to the theory that divers are not always aware of their true impairment.

The deeper divers were taken, the less accurately they were able to predict how affected they were by narcosis even when their scores were close to that of surface levels. Divers were also less confident in their ability and there was a noted delay to perform a task the deeper the depth of the test.

The results of the tests showed that narcosis is not simply an objective measurable phenomenon. Narcosis has a significant subjective component and is affected by numerous factors that include experience, age, gender, motivation, heat, social psychology, personal belief, the rate of descent, time of day, PPO2, PPN2 and PPCO2. It should be noted that even though some divers did not fare far worse at depth than at the surface, the confidence level for more cognitively demanding tasks is lower, including diver reaction time to perform tasks.

Oxygen narcosis

Oxygen itself is around 1.7 times as narcotic as Nitrogen. This is not normally a problem as the percentage of Oxygen is reduced on deep dives, thus lowering the Oxygen's narcotic effect. However, at elevated partial pressures (around 1.8 ata) Oxygen can dramatically exacerbate symptoms of Nitrogen narcosis. The reactions to high PPO2 are complex and the amount of Nitrogen and possibly Helium in the breathing mix is seen to have an effect. Although few people would plan a dive with a PPO2 this high, many divers (often untrained divers) do deep air bounce dives in excess of 240 ft where the PPO2 would approach and exceed these levels.

Oxygen DCS

Oxygen starts to behave as an inert gas and can produce Oxygen DCS normally at 2 atm and over PPO2, although sometimes seen at pressures below 1.7 atm. For high partial pressures of O2, O2 bubbles can form at deeper depths, however symptoms are normally only seen after dives with very long decompression stops on pure O2 or close to pure O2. Symptoms normally include severe acute joint pain that manifest within minutes after surfacing.

Oxygen DCS symptoms normally disappear relatively quickly by themselves and are thought to be due to Oxygen-filled bubbles. The bubbles are thought to be quickly absorbed into the surrounding tissue, lessening the pressure on pain receptors that results in a disappearance of the symptoms.

Cutis Marmorata

Cutis marmorata is a skin rash and a manifestation of DCS. This can be from omitting decompression stops or making inadequate decompression. However, in deep diving it can occur due to isobaric counter diffusion from having a different gas in one's drysuit than the inspired gas. Gas is absorbed through the skin and can cause from a slight skin rash to a heavy skin rash and even DCS on long exposures. The rash normally starts with erythema (from the Greek erythros, meaning red and is redness of the skin) and pruritus (sensation that causes the desire or reflex to scratch) followed by the developing of a mottled appearance and can include areas of pallor surrounded by cyanotic patches. Recompression normally resolves the rash.

CNS Oxygen toxicity

Oxygen under elevated pressures can become toxic. Partial pressure exposure to more than 160 KPa or about 1.6 ata can result in convulsions. However, breathing Oxygen at partial pressures above 60 KPa or around 0.6 ata for extended periods can result in permanent pulmonary fibrosis. The alveoli in the lungs start to dry out and their ability to transfer gas in and out declines. The first two cases of Oxygen toxicity in man were reported by British scientist Thomson in 1935 where two men breathed Oxygen at 4 ata.

High PPO2 over a short time can result in CNS toxicity, which symptoms include muscle convulsions, visual disturbances, nausea, twitching (normally in facial muscles), ears ringing (tinnitus), and irritability. Note, cases have been reported of CNS toxicity with convulsion when breathing PPO2 as low as 1.31 ata for ½ hour. Interestingly, individuals who suffer from epilepsy subjected to high pressures of Oxygen did not demonstrate a greater sensitivity towards the effects of high PPO2.

Long exposures over 0.5 ata can result in damage to the lungs and difficulty breathing, to permanent lung damage. To track the Oxygen exposure one must track both CNS toxicity and OTU or UPTD. An OTU (Oxygen tolerance unit) or UPDT (unit of pulmonary toxic dose) is basically breathing 1 PPO2 for 1 minute. However, it is not a sliding scale, as 1.3 PPO2 is not equal to 1.3 OTU.

Even at long decompression stops on high PPO2, vassal constriction followed by pulmonary edema occurs and both breathing and off-gassing are affected. Many divers elect to decompress on EAN70 to EAN80 rather than pure O2 to lessen the effects. Alternatively, divers will take air breaks of about 5 minutes on air every 20 to 25 minutes of O2 decompression.

Facial pallor is thought to be due to an expression of the intense peripheral vasoconstriction due to the excess Oxygen. Fasciculation (twitching) of the face and lips was noted in dry chamber dives before convulsions, but not always underwater. Strangely, changing to an air mixture from O2 in some cases brought on a sudden onset of a convulsion, thought to be due to the sudden drop in Oxygen supply to the intoxicated nerve cells.

When diving on a rebreather on long dives, many divers elect to keep the PPO2 low at 1 to 1.3. However, it can be needed to drop the PPO2 below 0.7 on long decompression stops, helping the body to more effectively off-gas by limiting vasoconstriction and bronchi constriction.

In tests with Drosophila fruit flies, it was seen that wing beating was reduced for one day after a short exposure to Oxygen at 7 ata. With a 40-minute exposure, the effects do not diminish in some cases up to four days after exposure. If a second exposure is followed directly after the first however, it resulted in the death of the fly. Recovery of toxic effects seems to be fast in the first stages. Tests on guinea pigs showed toxic effects after five hours of O2 at 3 ata. With breaks of 7% O2 every 30 minutes for seven minutes, toxic effects were only noted after 20-hour exposure (15 hours overall O2 exposure). This forms the basis for taking O2 breaks during decompression, or to use a lower EANx mix for decompression.

For interest, long term Oxygen exposure reduces life expectancy, but reduced Oxygen levels do not increase life expectancy, air seems to be best. The fruit flies had a reduced lifespan of 50% when subjected to 37% Oxygen and even at 21% Oxygen (marginally higher than air).

During metabolism, cells use Oxygen to produce adenosine triphosphate (ATP) in mitochondria (subcellular organelles producing energy for the cells) to create energy in stored form. In the production of ATP, electrons are transferred to O2 by cytochrome enzymes contained in the membrane of mitochondria. However, elevated pressures of Oxygen reduce metabolism.

Occasionally in the process of creating ATP, electrons escape and can combine with free molecular Oxygen to form a superoxide radical. Due to the Oxygen gaining an electron it has an unpaired electron. This superoxide can be converted to hydrogen peroxide and water by the enzyme superoxide dismutase. Hydrogen peroxide is highly toxic and reactive. Note this is a normal occurrence in daily life, however with increased PPO2 the number of superoxide radicals increases.

Two enzymes (catalase and glutathione peroxidase) in the brain detoxify hydrogen peroxide. These enzymes may become depleted during Oxygen stress as the enzymes are used up faster to detoxify the increased amount of hydrogen peroxide than the enzymes are replaced. Glutathione peroxidase reacts with hydrogen peroxide to form water and oxidized glutathione (GSSG). Hydrogen peroxide is seen to be a leading cause of seizures and it is recorded that hydrogen peroxide levels can increase by up to 700% when exposed to 3 ata O2. Note that although hydrogen peroxide gets naturally created in the brain it is at a lower level.

Although hydrogen peroxide is not particularly reactive it can be reduced to hydroxyl radical which is very reactive and toxic that can in turn react with cell lipids to form lipid peroxides, in addition to reacting with sulfhydryl groups in proteins to form disulfide bridges. These reactions alter fat cell membranes, cell receptors and enzyme functions that are thought to result in seizures. Interestingly, from studies on animals it was found that increased levels of vitamin E (α-tocopherol) increase the time to hyperoxic seizures, thus giving some protection. Hydrogen peroxide also affects brain amino acid levels, and it is known that elevated brain levels of excitatory amino acids cause seizures.

As a side note, some decongestants that contain pseudoephedrine and phenylpropanolamine can increase the risk of a seizure.

An elevation of partial pressures of Oxygen results in an elevation of free radicals found in the body, with partial pressures above 0.5 ata thought to be the limit where the body generally cannot cope with the amount of damage done by the free radicals. The repair process slowly starts to lag and given enough time, permanent damage can result. This is the reason for the exposure time limits to elevated partial pressure of Oxygen.

Here is a short exposure table.

PPO2	Max time in minutes
0.6	720
0.7	570
0.8	450
0.9	360
1	300
1.1	240
1.2	210
1.25	195
1.3	180
1.35	165
1.4	150
1.45	135
1.5	120
1.55	82
1.6	45

Oxygen does not combust itself. However, in the presence of high amounts of Oxygen, it promotes rapid combustion to other materials.

Normal Oxygen partial pressure is 0.20 to 0.21 ata at sea level. A partial pressure below this point is known as hypoxic. Below 0.16 ata signs and symptoms of hypoxia start to show, and below 0.1 ata unconsciousness and death can result. The general range for diving O2PP is 0.16 to 1.6 ata, although it can go as high as 3 ata in hyperbaric therapy (Oxygen of 3 ata at rest for one hour has been noted to be tolerated by most in chamber dives).

Although Oxygen has a narcosis level of 1.7 times Nitrogen, it is generally taken as 1 when computing END (equivalent narcotic depth) values. This is more for simplicity in calculation and due to the Oxygen level being normally less than the original level as in hypoxic mixes.

Breathing higher PPO2

It is thought that higher PPO2 causes an alteration to enzyme activity in the lungs with a loss of polyphosphatase activity in the pulmonary vessels. Vasal congestion followed by edema and lymphocytic infiltration have been noted within 10 minutes of breathing pure Oxygen (on the surface). A reduction in bronchial lumen further follows due to reabsorption of alveolar gas.

Atelectasis (a collapse of part or all of the lung) is seen after around 10 to 20 minutes of Oxygen breathing, and it is thought that this would not be seen if a small amount of narcotic gas was used in the breathing mix. Thus the cause of precocious atelectasis is seen to be due to the absence of inert gas in the breathing mix. Following then that bronchial obstruction is seen to be due to breathing high pressures of O2, and atelectasis (and reduction in lung volume) is due to the absence of inert gas, many divers elect to use EAN80 for the final decompression. The additional duration needed for decompression is minimal, however the advantages of switching to the gas deeper and decompressing deeper add to the reduced stress on the lungs in favor of not using pure O2 for decompression.

Interestingly, in tests by Dale and Rahn, a lung was inflated with air and sealed, and took six hours to collapse, seen to be due to the low membrane diffusion coefficient of Nitrogen. When they did the same test with a lung inflated with pure Oxygen, the lung deflated in six minutes. At altitude (0.26 ata), lung collapse on O2 was noted to take only one minute. In tests done by Workman, Bond and Mazzone no alteration in albino rats was found on a 3/97 Heliox mix after 14 days at 60 m (200 ft). However, when air was used death occurred after around 30 to 35 hours and is thought to be due to the high PPO2 inducing vasal congestion, edema, peribronchial infiltration, and a reduction in bronchial lumen.

Tests done to depths of 90 m (300 ft) using air, EAN 4/96 and Heliox 4/96 showed the following. The EANx and air mixture reduced ventilation under pressure even with exercise, with air having the greatest effect; the effect was not noted in the Helium mix. A second test at 30 m (100 ft) with EANx mixtures of 10, 40 and 60 % O2 was done. An increase in arterial CO2 pressure was noted in the higher Oxygen mixtures, while breathing both the EAN 4/96 and Heliox 4/96 mix at depth did not result in an increase in arterial CO2 pressure. Air on the other hand, only showed an increase in arterial CO2 pressure when activity was done compared to the higher Oxygen mixtures showing an increase even at rest. Showing that hyperoxia has a depressing effect on ventilation and venous return when at work.

This will lead to retention of CO_2 if the diver is working while breathing a high PPO2 (O2 saturates the hemoglobin that would have transported CO_2). The amount of retention depends on the work the diver does, the fitness of the diver and the PPO2. It should be noted that lowered heart rate, lung volume change due to bronchi constriction, and reduction in metabolism occurs immediately when PPO2 exceeds 0.5 ata, although to a small degree at this level, with the effects increasing as the PPO2 increases.

Divers sometimes experience headaches when diving on EANx mixes, especially if the diver is unfit or needs to swim against a current. This can often be contributed to the retention of CO_2 by the diver. Although it can also be due to the trigger point for breathing for the diver not being the level of CO_2 in the body but the level of O2. Thus with a higher level of O2 due to pressure, the trigger to breathe may be delayed long enough for CO_2 to build up and result in CO_2 poisoning. In these cases divers normally do not have headaches when diving on air to the same depth where they had headaches on EANx mixes.

For interest, it was found that elevated PPO2 for deeper dives was not ideal, a lower PPO2 was more suitable. Better results were found on air dives to 100 ft (30 m) than on increased O2 mixes or increased N2 mixes for that matter. In tests on dives that included exercise and to depths of 100 m (300 ft) a 14% (1.54 ata O2) Oxygen mixture had some subjects terminate the dive while those that continued did so with very poor results. When the same dive was done on a 4% (0.44 ata O2) Oxygen mixture, very good results were seen.

It is the suggestion from researchers that mixtures that contain normal range Oxygen pressures (150 to 350 mm Hg, 0.2 to 0.47 ata O2) be used for the bottom part of the dive and only be elevated at the decompression part of the dive. Common practice for many tech divers is to use a 1.4 PPO2 for OC and 1.3 PPO2 for CCR for the bottom part, although some do lower it to 1.2 PPO2 for OC and 1 PPO2 for CCR on very long dives. It should further be noted that since CCR units keep the PPO2 constant during ascent (assuming normal operation and ascent speed), a lower PPO2 is sometimes used compared to OC as the PPO2 drops on ascent for OC until the diver changes to a mix containing a higher fraction of O2, thus total O2 toxicity would be less.

The table on the following page shows the response to breathing different pressures of Oxygen and was originally sourced from a report (ONR Report DR-150) Principles and Observation on the Physiology of the Scuba Diver, however it has been altered to fit the scope of this book with additions from other sources.

PIO2 Mm H	PAO2 Mm Hg	Body response
58	30	Decreased heart rate, lung hypoventilation, circulatory collapse, convulsions and unconsciousness
65	36	Hypertension, increased heart rate, lung hyperventilation, reflex excitement, mental confusion
80	45	Lung hyperventilation, increased heart rate, hypertension, dysphoria, attention loss, critical discernment
100	60	Lung hyperventilation, increased heart rate, chemoreceptor increases electrical activity
120	80	Normal range
350	310	The upper limit of normal O2 range, also limit seen as safe for long term elevated PPO2 exposure such as saturation diving
364	324	Depressive circulatory, respiratory and metabolic threshold
713	673	Constriction and congestion in lung vessels, inhibition of polyphosphate activity in lungs
1000	960	Lowered heart rate (around 10 to 14%), lowered systolic and pulse pressure, CO2 retention, respiratory feedback depression, decreases in pH with an increase in lactate and RQ output. Max limit thought safe for medium depths with up to one hour work.
1170	1130	Possibility of CNS symptoms such as convulsions, especially if doing heavy underwater work (PPO2 1.6 ata = 1200 mm Hg)
1473	1433	Max limit for cerebral lipid peroxides
1600	1560	Neuronol hyper excitability, neurotoxic limit for underwater work
2200	2160	Max limit for resting individuals in water 64.4 °F (18 °C)
2500	2460	Max limit for resting individuals in a dry chamber

-Iron level changes

NASA recently quantified physiological changes in divers which were previously detected in astronauts in outer space by doing research on divers in an underwater habitat (off the coast of Florida) on a nearly two-week saturation dive at 19 m.

A decrease in hemoglobin and hematocrit with an increase in body iron and serum iron levels was detected in the divers and is thought to be due to an exposure to elevated levels of O2.

It is thought that the increased Oxygen pressure indirectly causes neocytolysis (destruction) of newly formed red blood cells. Red blood cells carry hemoglobin protein that binds to iron in addition to transporting O2. With the destruction of red blood cells, iron is released into free form that can cause the formation of free radicals which in turn damages DNA and proteins in addition to high levels of iron leading to liver cirrhosis, liver cancer, cardiomyopathy, diabetes and cataracts to name a few. An iron overload can produce closely the same symptoms as anemia (low iron levels).

A follow-up study from NASA showed that the divers' iron levels took about three months to return to normal. Although few divers do saturation dives of these lengths, divers who dive a lot have had similar results with high iron levels. Martin Kirk, a PADI divemaster, developed iron overload after working as a divemaster for seven months in Palau on a live-aboard logging 315 dives. He documented his cases on the internet after contacting DAN and NASA with months of research to solve his iron level problems.

Divers making multiple dives a day continuously (as dive guides, instructors and divemasters do) should be aware of the potential risk to iron overload.

-Blood restriction
High pressures of Oxygen also modify collagen tissue (a group of naturally-occurring proteins), interfering with circulation and nutrition to bone tissue. Bones are life cells that are connected by collagen tissue. High pressures of Oxygen also cause fat cells to swell, raising the internal pressure in the bone and possibly cutting off blood supply by constricting blood vessels.

-Air breaks
On long decompression schedules with Oxygen it is sometimes necessary that air breaks (or a switch to another gas with lower O2) are needed to give the body a rest period. This is to reverse some of the effects of breathing high PPO2. Many divers do not count the time spent on air (or other gas) as part of the decompression time and are correct in doing so as off-gassing is slowed down. Air breaks are normally either taken as 5 minutes on air for every 20 minutes on O2 or 2 ½ minutes on air for every 10 minutes on O2. However, what divers often forget is the O2 payback time. Switching back to a gas with a higher percentage of inert gas will result in some on-gassing, which needs to be accounted for on decompression.

NASA has protocols for taking air breaks in their space programs and these differ depending on the length of the air break and if the person is exercising or at rest. For air breaks with the person at rest payback time is double the time of the air break and if the break is longer than 10 minutes the whole Nitrogen elimination schedule for the astronaut needs repeating.

Various other schedules are in place depending on the situation, and payback time can be as high as 35 times the air break time. Although it should be noted that these procedures are worked out for air breaks, changing to different gasses to do decompression O2 breaks will alter the situation, the diver should still be aware that on-gassing will occur and that some compensation for it should be allowed by increasing the total decompression time.

It is known that breathing 1 ata of O2 decreases cardiac output and increases peripheral vascular resistance due to vasoconstriction, thus it is reasonable to suppose asymmetrical Nitrogen kinetics as a consequence of air breaks, in addition to supposing that a change in the size distribution of tissue micronuclei results due to a change in the O2 window on air breaks.

Tests done by Pilmanis on NASA astronauts showed that a 10-minute air break occurring 30 minutes into a one hour deNitrogenation schedule for a 4.37 psia exposure reduced the time to the onset of symptoms, in addition to increasing DCS incidence, compared to controls.

Helium narcosis

Breathing pure Helium can lead to asphyxia and death. The Helium found in balloons is required by many countries to have 20% Oxygen in the mix. A common party trick is to breathe the gas from the Helium filled balloons to create a Donald Duck voice effect.

Few people realize that Helium is in fact narcotic. This is due to the low narcosis of Helium. Helium only starts to show in calculations at a greater percentage (normally above 50%) and at greater depth (normally below 250 ft).

Another problem with Helium and deep diving is that Helium removes heat from the diver's body on deep dives. Put another way, Helium has a greater heat conductivity and each Helium molecule can carry more heat away than Nitrogen molecules. But, there are fewer molecules per volume of gas compared to Nitrogen, so the effect is only noted when the pressure goes up and sufficiently increases the density of the gas.

Commercial divers get around this problem by heating the breathing gas, but technical divers do not normally have this option.

Divers at shallower depths, around 200 to 300 ft (60 to 90 m), may report feeling colder than on a deep air dive, but this is believed to be due to the narcosis level of deep air dives. The Helium density at this depth is not normally enough to chill the diver, the diver is just more aware of the cold when breathing a Helium mix rather than air.

The critical depth is normally in the range of 825 to 924 ft (250 to 280 m). This is the range where the Helium in the mix removes more heat than the body is capable of producing. On deep saturation dives, the gas is normally heated to around 86 °F (30 °C) to keep the divers warm.

Helium does not dissolve into your tissue at the same rate as Nitrogen due to it being less soluble than Nitrogen. However, being a thinner gas, the Helium that does dissolve into your tissue does so faster than Nitrogen. In short, Helium is more diffusible than Nitrogen but less soluble. All in all, Helium has 2.645 times faster half times (M value) than Nitrogen.

Due to the faster half life of Helium, decompression for short deep dives (bounce dives) on Helium can be longer than if no Helium was used, due to the fast on-gassing of the Helium in a short time. However, for saturation diving, decompression on Helium mixtures would be shorter, due to Helium being less soluble than Nitrogen and its faster off-gassing rate. For the normal technical diver the dives done are mostly seen as bounce dives or short deep dives. This is why some people still prefer deep air dives, as the decompression can be less than that of a Helium mixture dive, and calculations are simpler.

Hyperbaric bradycardia and tachycardia

It was noted that breathing Nitrogen mixes under pressure caused hyperbaric bradycardia (reduction in heart rhythm) under elevated partial pressures. This had the result of reduced cardiac output with lowered arterial pressure. 1 mg of atropine prevented hyperbaric bradycardia. Tests done in 1963 at 264 ft (80 m) with an EAN 4/96 mixture showed arterial hypotension with a reduction of amplitude and rate of pulse in addition to a slowing of venous return.

From tests done on Helium mixes starting in the 1960s it was found that Helium mixes reduced hyperbaric bradycardia (reduced heart rate) normally found with Air and EANx mixtures. Helium mixes in fact caused tracycardia (an increased heart rate and arterial pressure) at shallower depths with subjects at rest until a high enough pressure was reached to allow the Helium to reach a density and narcotic effect large enough to cause an increase in respiratory resistance, were heart rate lowered again.

The deviation was reasonably constant for subjects breathing Nitrogen mixtures with a decrease of around 11 beats/minute at 90 m (300 ft) and a decrease of 10 mm Hg systolic pressure, in addition to a general reduction in diastolic pressure. Breathing a Helium mix saw an increase of around 10 beats/minute, with an increase of systolic and diastolic pressure of around 7 mm Hg.

However, with higher Oxygen contents the reduced heart rate almost doubled, at 30 m (100 ft) breathing an EAN 10/90 resulted in an average reduction of 5 beats/minute, while breathing EAN 60/40 had an almost double reduction in heart rate, thus higher PPO2 reduces heart rate, stroke volume, slowing down venous blood return, and lowering of arterial blood pressure. This may be due to high PPO2 affecting the chemoreceptors that inhibits the reaction of the baroceptors, Oxygen at high pressures also depresses metabolism.

High pressure nervous syndrome (HPNS)

High pressure nervous syndrome (HPNS) is a neurological and physiological diving disorder found in deep Helium dives. It is believed that the surrounding pressure that the diver is at is the actual problem and not the Helium in the mix.

-HPNS history

Royal Navy physiologist Peter B. Bennett (founder of Divers Alert Network) was the first to describe HPNS symptoms in English publications (1965). Brauer was the first to use the term high pressure nervous syndrome. HPNS was coined as a term to describe the combined symptoms that occurred in a 1,189 ft chamber dive in Marseilles at the time. However, Russian scientist G. L. Zal'tsman did experiments on deep dives and also reported the same symptoms from his experiments (1961).

-Depth of symptoms

HPNS normally occurs at depths in excess of 500 ft (151 m) when using mixes that contain high Helium percentages, such as Heliox, although some divers have experienced light signs of HPNS on Heliox mixtures at depths in the range of 264 ft (80 m) on fast descents.

It is generally thought that the limit for Heliox is in the range of 660 ft (200 m) and that HPNS is a concern for every diver below 1000 ft even if breathing Tri-Mix (O2, He, N2). Alternative gasses will be needed to safely dive below 1000 ft. In tests on rats it was found that when core temperatures were lowered, the subjects became more resistant to tremors and seizures.

In the hypothermic group (mean colon temp of 27.4 Celsius) no seizures were found even at 4500 fsw (max pressure reachable by the test chamber), where hyperthermic rats (mean colon temp 40 Celsius) had symptoms at 2450 fsw, while the control group (mean colon temp 37.2 Celsius) had symptoms at 3700 fsw.

-HPNS symptoms

Divers may experience muscle twitching, micro sleep, tremors, somnolence, electroencephalography (EEG) changes, myoclonic jerking, visual disturbance, nausea, vomiting, dizziness, and decreased mental performance with the severity and onset being individual dependent.

-HPNS solution

By adding Nitrogen (about 5 to 10%) or Hydrogen (creating Hydreliox) into the mix and slowing descent rate helps to reduce symptoms and prevent large initial decrements in performance, being the primary protocol used in saturation diving. Although alcohol, some anesthetics and anticonvulsant drugs have had successes in tests on animals in suppressing HPNS, none are currently used in diving. The use of 5-HT1A receptor antagonists can provide some prevention of HPNS but needs further research before commercial use.

From tests done by the Department of Physiology and Anesthesia, Duke Medical Centre it was found that for dives to 1000 ft, 1 atm N2 for every 9 atm Helium is needed to prevent HPNS symptoms and would require about 10% Nitrogen for a dive to 31 ata (1000 ft). For the same depth only 0.5% of Nitrous Oxide would be required and 29% Hydrogen would be required to prevent HPNS symptoms (16% Hydrogen was calculated, but tests showed around 29% was needed).

Hydreliox is a mixture of Hydrogen, Helium and Oxygen. Hydrogen is easier to breathe than Helium at depth and is also cheaper. However, Hydrogen becomes explosive if mixed with more than 5.3% Oxygen, thus it is normally only used in very deep dives where the Oxygen percentage is 4% or lower.

Comex did tests in 1989 where divers used Hydreliox to 1742 ft in the ocean and reported that breathing was about the same as breathing Heliox at 800 ft. Divers also reported feeling less tired and had fewer HPNS symptoms. Hydrogen in the mixture however does increase decompression time and due to the explosion risk, the gas requires different protocols than Helium only gas mixes, making it more expensive and difficult to use.

Another solution is to use intravenous drugs such as urethane, ethanol and Phenobarbital. Urethane is effective at preventing tremors, while Phenobarbital is effective at preventing tonic convulsions. Depths of 8,250 fsw were reached with a compression rate of 60 Atm/hr with excellent results (on animals). Staged compression with adaption stop times at certain depths has seen excellent results. A staged reduction in compression speed is sometimes used in deep diving where initial compression is fast to around 500 ft (150 m), followed by slower and slower compression speed as the depth increases.

-What happens

HPNS is believed to be due to the pressure at these depths compressing the lipid cells (mostly dopamine pathways) so much as to interfere with spinal cord transmission due to Helium not having the same effect on the lipid cells as Nitrogen to allow them to expand to counter the pressure. As Nitrogen dissolves into cells under pressure, it causes the cell to expand, causing narcosis. Due to Helium being less soluble than Nitrogen, less Helium molecules will diffuse into a cell at a given pressure, thus causing less expansion pressure. At depth, the ambient pressure is enough to compress the cells causing the opposite effects of narcosis, interfering in neuron pathways. Since the Helium in the cells does not cause enough outward pressure to offset the ambient pressure compression on the cells, Nitrogen is added to offset the compression effect. Normally Nitrogen at an amount from 5 to 10% is enough to create a pressure in the cells to withstand ambient pressure compression.

From studies on guinea pigs it was noted that increased pressure exerted a significant suppressive effect on the depolarization induced calcium dependent release of glycine and GABA by the spinal cord presynaptic nerve terminals. It is noted that pressure can affect multiple pathways from the brain to the body which control involuntary movement. The pressure affecting the synaptic transmission between the neurons in the central nervous system is thought to be the cause of the tremors.

Gas induced osmosis also possibly plays a part in HPNS. Water can shift between different tissue compartments under pressure and can cause mechanical disruption, gas diffusion changes, plasma loss, possible bubble formation, and hemoconcentration, to name a few. With rapid pressure changes the gas in blood and tissue may not equilibrate fast enough and a counter fluid pressure gradient (osmotic gradient) may result.

-HPNS nausea cause

To find the cause of nausea in HPNS, three divers were studied in chamber dives to 720 and 1000 ft with Heliox and Tri-Mix as breathing gas. Dizziness and nausea were not found to be due to changes in vestibular function, but rather due to a decrease in the normal cerebellar inhibitory modulation of the brain stem vestibular nuclei. This would result in an increased impulse frequency over the right and left central vestibular connections, causing ocular and limb tremor and nausea.

-First use of Tri-Mix for dives to 1000 ft to eliminate HPNS

To try to reduce HPNS and the time of descent (up to then descent time to 1000 ft took 6 to 8 days to prevent HPNS), Nitrogen was added to the mix. The first tests were done on tadpoles and later mice, followed by manned dives at the Duke Medical Center in 1974. The descent time was only 33 minutes to 1000 ft with no signs of HPNS.

CO poisoning

CO binds to other molecules including myoglobin and mitochondrial cytochrome oxidase and CO exposure is damaging to the heart and CNS system.

CO bonds about 200 to 225 times more regularly with blood cells than Oxygen and keeps clinging to the cells, blocking the body's ability to take up Oxygen and remove CO_2. The combination with hemoglobin is called carboxyhemoglobin. Smokers constantly take in CO and one cigarette can affect the diver's gas transport ability for hours. A single cigarette can cut a diver's lung volume down to as low as 50% for an hour or more. This can compromise decompression stops by making them inadequate due to limiting gas transport. Since all smokers have a degree of lung damage, it places smokers at higher risk for lung rupture injuries, especially when shallow deco needs to be done in rough conditions. Lung damage can also increase the amount of lung shunting and can degrade the lungs' ability to filter out venous bubbles that may then be passed to the arterial side. Increased levels of CO also reduce the tolerance for high PPO2.

Symptoms of CO poisoning include headache, nausea, vomiting, dizziness, fatigue, weakness, confusion, disorientation, syncope, possible seizures, retinal hemorrhages, cyanosis, possible unconsciousness, and death.

CO2 poisoning

In diving, CO2 retention can be a problem and can lead to CO2 poisoning, which symptoms can range from heavy breathing, headaches, nausea to unconsciousness or blackout.

CO2 is converted to bicarbonate to help the body maintain a normal pH balance. About 75% of the CO2 in the body is converted to carbonic acid (H_2CO_3) which can be converted to bicarbonate (HCO_3-) when needed. Excess CO2 is expelled from the body and receptors (chemoreceptors) in the arch of the aorta and throughout the arteries send signals to the respiratory center that allows it to control your breathing and in turn control the level of PCO2 in the arterial blood, being from 35 to 45 mmHg at rest (average 40 mmHg) with venous blood being about 45 mmHg. A level above 45 mmHg will result in a marked increase in respiration. PaCO2 of around 50-60 mmHg significantly reduces both mental and physical skills performance.

Around 80% of the Oxygen consumed is converted to CO2, with the remaining 20% converted to water. As Oxygen consumption increases, more CO2 is produced, triggering ventilation to supply more Oxygen and eliminate the additional CO2 produced.

Prolonged exposure to moderate concentrations can cause acidosis as well as an adverse effect on calcium phosphorus metabolism, resulting in an increase in calcium deposits in soft tissues. CO2 is toxic to the heart and can affect the heart's ability to contract, the higher the percentage of CO2 in the breathing mix the more adverse the effect. CO2 is around 130 times as narcotic as Nitrogen.

1% can cause drowsiness after prolonged exposures.
2% causes mild narcosis, increased blood pressure, higher pulse rate and reduced hearing.
5% causes difficulty breathing, dizziness, confusion, headache and shortness of breath, and possibly panic.
8% causes headache, sweating, dim vision, tremor and loss of consciousness after exposure of five to ten minutes.

Note that these are percentages based on partial pressures when the diver is at 1 atm and that when diving to depth a smaller percentage of CO2 will reach the same partial pressure as a larger percentage on the surface.

In pressure this equates to:
PCO2 above 70-75 mmHg reduces the level of awareness.
PaCO2 above 100-120 mmHg produces unresponsiveness.
PaCO2 220 to 300 mmHg produces surgical anesthesia and seizures.
These levels are for 1 ata, at depth the effect is more pronounced. In tests done by Haldane, subjects lost consciousness and some seized at PaCO2 just over 100 mmHg at 300 fsw.

In tests that Warkander did on CO2 accumulation, two subjects had to be rescued (from a wet pot) while exercise at 6.8 ata (around 191 ft) while not being aware that they were incapacitated. Their arterial PCO2 was above 80-90 mmHg.

A poorly tuned regulator cannot only cause pulmonary barotrauma or edema, but also CO2 retention and a higher work of breathing that produces even more CO2. For long dives, CO2 exposure must be kept below 5 mbars, normal level is around 5.2 kPa, 0.052 ata or 39 mmHg. 6.2 kPa is the upper limit of the normal range, over 8.5 kPa sudden incapacitation is highly likely. Experiments done on working divers found a level between 6.5 to 7.5 kPa not to be uncommon. A diver (especially if unfit) working against a current can easily reach these values.

When breathing elevated partial pressures of Oxygen, higher levels of Oxygen dissolve into the blood and tissues and limit the ability of the blood to transport CO2 out of the tissues. This results in higher venous and tissue CO2 levels than would normally be found in the body. The result can be a build-up of CO2 that can over time lead to CO2 poisoning. This could be as a result of using a rebreather at a higher PPO2 (normally 1.3) while working hard, working hard at depth on air (deep air), or needing to swim against a current on a high deco mix. It was noted by Asmussen and Neilsen in tests that sudden change to higher PO2 caused a rapid drop in ventilation, thus changing to a deco mix while fighting a current can suddenly build up CO2 due to reduced ventilation.

Skip breathing, poorly tuned regulators and poor quality regulators which are hard to breathe from and hard work, will increase the amount of CO2 produced by the body. This will further complicate your dive by increasing Nitrogen narcosis and the risk of getting decompression sickness, and can cause Oxygen toxicity symptoms at lower levels of PPO2 than is normally a problem, as CO2 lowers your tolerance for O2 toxicity.

Anton Swanepoel

Higher than normal levels of CO_2 in the body will cause a diver's breathing to increase and use up the available gas supply faster. By breathing faster the diver may over breathe a regulator and get the feeling of being starved of gas or not getting enough gas. The diver may start to panic and this in turn will increase narcosis, breathing, CO_2 production (forming a loop), susceptibility to CNS toxicity and decompression sickness. If the diver does not realize something is wrong and correct their breathing, a disaster may not be far off.

CO_2 poisoning symptoms include rapid breathing, shortness of breath, headache (normally throbbing or severe), dizziness, confusion, nausea, visual problems, tremors, muscle twitching, convulsions, unconsciousness and death.

It is noted that a rapid increase of CO_2 can cause blackouts without any warning and can result from working hard when swimming against a current on the surface, poor breathing habits, contaminated gas with high levels of CO_2 in, or hard breathing regulators (building up CO_2) and then making a rapid descent. It should be noted that on descent, the gas volume in the lungs will be reduced due to ambient pressure increase. Thus, the amount of exhaled gas will be lower than would have been the case had the diver remained at a constant depth.

With each breath on descent a residual amount of gas will remain in the lungs. This amount of gas contains unventilated CO_2 and the faster the descent is, the higher the percentage of CO_2 will become in the residual gas volume. Should the percentage of CO_2 already have been high on the surface before descending, CO_2 poisoning is highly likely. The speed of descent is thus very important and a rate of 66 ft (20 m)/minute is seen to be the max one should descend at. CO_2 build-up is made more likely if the diver makes shallow breaths as dead airspace is percentage wise increased when compared to inhaled volume size, especially with a fast descent rate. See dead airspace section for more detail.

Elevated levels of CO_2 cause the blood vessels to dilate and have multiple effects on the body, including predisposing the diver to hyperoxic seizures, reduced mental and physical abilities, and increased narcosis. Dilated blood vessels will cause more inert gas to be dissolved into the tissues quicker and can pre-dispose a diver to decompression sickness.

The CO_2 can increase any bubbles already found in tissues or blood and compound matters even more. The increase of blood flow to the skin and tissues can increase heat loss. This can not only potentially lead to chilling the diver, but gas dissolves per volume into a colder tissue more than when warm (warm beer loses its bubbles as it heats up) and can result in the diver on-gassing even more inert gas and pre-dispose him/her even more to decompression sickness.

Due to CO_2 being around 25 times more soluble than O_2, a large amount of CO_2 is dissolved in the blood, thus to drop the level of CO_2 even a small amount one needs to remove a large amount of CO_2 from the body. To remove this large amount of CO_2, ventilation needs to be increased. However, at depth increased gas density will limit ventilation ability.

When lung ventilation rate increases, exhaling effort increases, and progressive increase in the force of exhalation will increase the gas flow rate only up to a maximum point. Due to increased ambient pressure underwater, the airways can be compressed and collapsed, obstructing the gas flow out of the lungs. The amount of gas that can be expelled out of the lungs is limited by the collapse of the airways and the fact that the airways collapse at a lower gas flow expiratory rate the denser the gas is, which results in the maximal possible lung ventilation per minute progressively reducing as gas density increases.

Thus it gets harder and harder to clear excess CO_2 from the body the deeper the diver descends, and the ability to maintain a normal $PaCO_2$ may not be possible when breathing a dense gas, especially if the diver is working. Maximum expiratory gas flow rate on air at 99 fsw is half what it would be on the surface. Increased CO_2 levels will in itself cause narcosis, and when the level rises to ±100 mmHg mental capacity is reduced in addition to the respiratory process being depressed, causing further CO_2 retention and increased $PaCO_2$ due to reducing lung ventilation. Thus a diver could become incapacitated without knowing it (as seen from the two divers that had to be rescued on the test mentioned before) and will continue to accumulate CO_2 until unconsciousness occurs.

Swimming at around 50-60 ft/minute a diver would normally require a ventilation rate of around 0.6 cu ft/minute for a fit diver and around 1 cu ft/minute for an unfit diver. Maximum ventilation at around 100 ft is around 3 to 3.5 cu ft/minute, however divers would normally only be able to sustain around 2.7 cu ft/minute (75%) of that over time.

Anton Swanepoel

If ventilation exceeds 1 cu ft/minute, especially over 2 cu ft /minute CO_2 accumulation is highly likely (note values are surface values). Tests done by Lanphier on US Navy divers swimming at about 75 ft/min showed an abnormal elevation of PCO_2, averaging 55 mmHg and divers breathing air at 7.8 ata (around 224 ft) during exertion rapidly lost consciousness.

Divers who consciously reduce their rate of ventilation in order to conserve gas may reduce ventilation to the point that they accumulate CO_2. When stressed, a person's metabolic rate is increased, which in turn will increase CO_2 production.

An interesting observation made by the author was when doing CCR dives on an Evolution unit that has an indicator to indicate the amount of scrubber used. Since CO_2 reacts with the scrubber material and creates heat in the process, a temperature sensitive measuring stick can be placed in the scrubber. As the scrubber material is used up, parts of the scrubber will thus be colder and be shown as used. On a normal dive of around 2 ½ hours duration (depth has little effect on scrubber usage) the author normally uses around one to max two bars of the scrubber as indicated on the display. On a dive where there was a heavy current the author used two bars of the scrubber within 45 minutes of the dive. This is a marked increase of CO_2 production.

Note that higher levels of O_2 aggravate the toxic effect of high pressures of CO_2. Increased levels of CO_2 on the other hand reduce the tolerance for high pressures of O_2 and are thought to be the result of the narcotic effect of the gas in addition to depression of neuron activity, as even the shift of pH towards acidity can affect the enzyme activity of Oxygen.

Note on rebreathers with CO_2 sensors, the sensor measures the amount of CO_2 in the loop and not in the diver's body.

Isobaric counter diffusion (ICD)

Isobaric Counter Diffusion (ICD) is a physiological effect where diffusion of different inert gases in different directions (on- and off-gassing) can produce or incite bubble formation, and the effect can occur without a change in surrounding ambient pressure.

ICD can increase gas elimination or interfere with gas elimination in decompression depending on gasses used and where the gas switches are made.

Although the basic concept of ICD is the same, different computers or desktop software will give different warnings for the same dive profile due to each algorithm following a different safety factor (explained later), this may cause a bit of confusion for some people. This section will hopefully clear up the confusion as to why different computers allow different gas switches.

-ICD History
ICD was first noted in a study where subjects breathed a Neon-Oxygen-Helium mix and then a Nitrogen-Helium-Oxygen mix while being saturated in a Helium environment at pressures equivalent to between 400 and 1200 fsw.

In diving, a common practice in the 1980s to early 2000 was to switch from a gas containing a high percentage of inert gas, normally Helium, to either air or a Nitrox blend with no Helium in the mix. The thought was to get off the Helium as quickly as possible. It was assumed that inert gas does not on- and off-gas separately and that the sum of the partial pressures of the gas must make up the whole of the ambient pressure.

Thus it was thought that if one was saturated with one gas, another gas cannot diffuse into the tissues until the first one off-gassed completely. Tests done in 1975 by Lambertsen and Iicula found that different gasses diffuse into the tissues independently of the other gasses around them and have little or no effect on each other.

Now it is becoming more common practice to switch to a lighter Tri-Mix blend.

-The problem
The reason for the effect of ICD is due to different inert gasses (such as Helium and Nitrogen) having a different rate of diffusion (speed they enter and exit the body), in addition that one gas will not take up the space of another gas in the body if you change the inspired gas, and that the gasses diffuse in and out of the body independently of each other without affecting each other.

-Types of ICD
There are two main different types of ICD to contend with: Superficial and Deep Tissue. Superficial counter diffusion is a form of ICD that is a problem when inspired gas differs from the gas in contact with the diver's skin. Deep Tissue ICD occurs when different inert gases are breathed in sequence, such as switching to different travel mixes or deco mixes. Note that both types of ICD can either occur at the same time during a dive or independently of each other.

Anton Swanepoel

-Superficial counter diffusion

Superficial counter diffusion occurs when the breathing mix contains a different mix than the gas in contact with the diver's skin, such as using Tri-Mix for breathing and Argon or air to inflate the drysuit, or where saturation divers breathe a different mix than what is in the chamber (using a mask to breathe a higher O2 content gas for decompression acceleration while chamber gas is different to lower fire risk and help with heat retention).

The inert gas will diffuse into the skin and a pressure difference between skin and tissue inert gas will result that can cause skin DCS. In helmet and chamber diving this is also a concern due to gas diffusing into the eardrum and forming bubbles in the inner ear that later can form venous bubbles, although only after long exposures.

In tests, subjects developed hard, raised, white cutaneous lesions that were bloodless. Experiments with pigs that were in a Helium environment while breathing different mixes containing either Nitrox, Neon-Oxygen or Argon-Oxygen led to skin bubbles that later led to tissue bubbles and later venous bubbles that in turn led to death from continuous venous gas embolism. It was determined from tests that the bubbles were formed due to inwards diffusion of Helium, not outwards diffusion of Helium, thus breathing a Heliox mix while surrounded by air did not produce the same effect.

Interestingly, breathing Nitrous Oxide in a Helium environment at 1 ata creates counter diffusion bubbles, and in tests with pigs the bubbles could cause death after exposure of only 1½ hours.

-Deep tissue counter diffusion

Deep tissue counter diffusion occurs when any different inert gasses are breathed in sequence, such as switching to different travel mixes or deco mixes or bailing out from a faulty CCR unit. There are two possibilities here, supersaturation or subsaturation.

--Supersaturation

In supersaturation a diver switches from a slower equilibrating inert gas to a higher equilibrating inert gas, for instance switching from a high Nitrogen mix (such as air) to a high Helium mix (such as Heliox). The higher equilibrating gas enters the tissues faster than the replaced inert gas leaves the tissue. Thus, the total pressure in the tissues will rise (this happens independent of depth changes). Any bubbles that are present have a higher chance of growing, including the added risk for additional bubbles forming.

An example is switching from air to 16/50 on descent at deep depths (200 ft) or after some time in shallow waters (swimming to a wall for 30 minutes at 60 ft on air before the switch). This switch is sometimes done due to using air as a travel gas for a deep dive. The effect of ICD here is because the Helium gas will diffuse faster into the tissues than the Nitrogen can diffuse out and the total pressure in the tissues will dramatically increase above ambient pressure.

-Subsaturation

Subsaturation is when a switch from a higher equilibrating inert gas to a lower equilibrating inert gas is made and is then a concern for mixed gas divers during gas switches and CCR divers bailing out to OC on rebreather malfunctions.

This is due to the new inert gas entering the tissue slower than the replaced inert gas leaving the tissue and thus the gradient for the faster inert gas is greater, thus speeding up the release of the inert gas. This can speed up decompression and is used in some technical, military, scientific and commercial diving. However, ICD is a concern when a gas switch is done where the percentage of inert gas in the new mix significantly differs from that of the mix switched from, for example, switching from a bottom mix of 18/50 to a 50% Nitrox mix at 70 fsw. This switch will increase the PPN2, causing the inspired pressure of Nitrogen to be higher than the previous mix and on-gassing will occur for the Nitrogen gas. This can cause a supersaturation pressure in the tissues that is over the critical trigger point and bubbles can form. The tissue's Helium pressure to inspired pressure will also significantly differ and a large supersaturation will result for the Helium gas, possibly leading to bubble formation.

Calculations for ICD DSC

The current thought is that you should not let the Nitrogen percentage go up more than 1% for every 5% Helium drop, with O2 taking up the rest of the 4%, or ideally have the O2 take up the full Helium drop, in addition to not making too large a drop in Helium (10 to 15% reduction is recommended).

Another point is that it is ideal to not switch gas on or just before a deep stop. Rather, do the deep stops then switch, or recalculate your switch point to be further away from a deep stop. This will minimize the chance of an ICD DCS hit.

Let's say you did a dive to 330 ft (100 m) with 12/65 on OC and you want to switch at 220 ft. You will be switching to 20% O2. That is an increase of 8% O2. Thus, we can allow the Nitrogen to go up 2%. Your mix would now be 20/55.

Anton Swanepoel

Now you want to switch at 98 ft, a 40% O2 will do. Since you upped the O2 by 20%, you can allow the Nitrogen to go up 5%.

The mix would now be 40/30.

Depending on your deco needs you can then change to an EAN80 at 33 ft, note some divers feel that it is better to decompress with a Heliox 80 (80% O2, 20 Helium) than an EAN80 mix if the dive was done with a high Helium percentage bottom mix. These changes will be smoother and easier on the body than switching to air at 220 ft and then to EAN32 and later EAN80 as was done before.

The reason for this is, if you allow the Nitrogen percentage to go up, the PPN2 in your body goes up, but you are not going deeper. That means that the PPN2 tension between what is in your tissues and the surrounding pressure increases. This could increase to a point that it can cause DCS at depth.

Let's look at the previous example of what would have happened to the Nitrogen and Helium if we did switch to air at 220 ft.

For the blend 12/65, we have 7.666 ata at 220 ft.
0.65 * 7.666 = 4.9829 atm for Helium
0.23 * 7.666 = 1.7631 atm for Nitrogen

Switching to air, we have 0 atm for Helium, as far as the Helium is concerned, you made a direct ascent from 220 ft in the time it took you to take that first breath of air. In addition, as we all know, Helium's density being a lot less than Nitrogen, it is a far less forgiving gas when it comes to depth changes. You get decompression sickness easier on Helium than on Nitrogen and normally worse as well.

The Nitrogen on the other hand increases to:
0.79 * 7.666 = 6.05614 atm Nitrogen
6.05614 / 1.7631 = 3.434 times the original PPN2 that you had in the mix. As far as narcosis goes, someone just switched off your lights.

-Differences between computers and desktop programs
Some dive computers and desktop software programs warn you when you try to make a gas switch that it thinks has a high risk for ICD. Confusion sometimes results due to the warnings not being consistent between them.

The reason for this is the same reason why different computers will allow you different bottom dive times, each works on the parameters that it was programmed for. One computer may allow only a 1% Nitrogen increase for every 5% Helium drop while other computers may allow no Nitrogen increase.

Some computers also calculate not only inspired gas percentage changes but also tissue pressure changes. If the computers use different half time tissue compartments then they will calculate different pressures for inert gasses in the tissue. Thus one algorithm may pick up a warning where another algorithm may not. For instance, if one computer uses a 2 minute half time and another computer only uses a 4 minute half time as its lowest value, the two will differ in their warnings.

The ratio in pressure change that they allow also can differ that will make two algorithms calculate warnings differently even if they use the same half times. For instance, if both algorithms use tissue half times of say 2, 4, 8, 12, 30, 60, 90, 200, 600, but the one calculates a max pressure difference allowable as a 1:2 ratio where the other calculates it as 1:1.58, then the warnings between them will differ.

The length of time spent at depth will allow larger tissue gas pressures and as a result will tolerate smaller changes in inspired gas percentages.

The following calculations are not 100% correct as other factors that affect diffusion are not included so as to simplify the explanation, however it is accurate enough for the examples given. Furthermore, note that the formulas used here are from my book 'Dive Computers' and readers are referred to it for a more in-depth explanation of the formulas used.
http://www.antonswanepoelbooks.com/dive_computers.php

For instance, using the Bühlmann's diffusion formula for half times we see the following results when using a tissue half time of 10 minutes.

Taking a breathing mixture of 20/45 at 200 ft we have the following calculations.

The diver has 0 pressure of Helium in the body at the start of the dive and if the descent took 4 minutes (50 ft/minute) then the diver will arrive with the following Helium pressure in the 10 minute compartment.

4 minute descent

$P_{comp} = 0 + [(3.177 - 0) /2] \times [1 - 2^{-4/10}]$

$P_{comp} = 0 + [1.5885] \times [0.24214]$

= 0.3846 atm Helium in 10 minute tissue compartment

If the diver were to now immediately switch to air, the inspired gas pressure drop for Helium would be 45% with an increase of 45% Nitrogen, which would seem large from our 1 to 5 drop rule, however since the pressure in the 10 minute tissue compartment is so small the pressure ratio drop would be small enough that the body can handle it.

After an hour dive things are a bit different.

$P_{comp} = 0.3846 + [(3.177 - 0.3846)] \times [1 - 2^{-60/10}]$

$P_{comp} = 0.3846 + [2.7924] \times [0.984375]$

= 3.13337 atm Helium in 10 minute tissue compartment

If we were to now switch to air, the resulting pressure difference would be very large and a high risk for ICD could result, possibly due to a CCR diver only taking air as a bailout for a 200 ft dive.

If we were to switch to a mix containing 20% Helium, the pressure of the inspired Helium would be 1.412 atm. 3.13337 / 1.412 = 2.2191, this would be a 2.2191 : 1 ratio. This can result from a CCR diver bailing out to a mix containing only 20% Helium, or an OC diver changing to a 20% Helium content gas. Although one would not normally do this, changing on ascent to a 20% Helium mix is sometimes done. As the pressure of the Helium in the tissues lessens on ascent, it is a matter of where the diver switches that will determine if there is an ICD risk or not.

Let's say the diver switches to a 30/20 Tri-Mix at 140 ft on the first stop, we have the following calculation. Taking ascent speed as 30 ft/minute, we have two minutes for ascent.

$P_{comp} = 3.13337 + [(2.3591 - 3.13337) /2] \times [1 - 2^{-4/10}]$

$P_{comp} = 3.13337 + [-0.387] \times [0.242142]$

= 3.03966 atm Helium when arriving at the stop in the 10 minute compartment.

3.03966 / 1.048485 = 2.8991 or a 2.8991 : 1 ratio for a 20% Helium mix, for a 30% Helium mix we have 3.03966 / 1.57273 = 1.93326 or a 1.93326 : 1 ratio.

We see then that dropping the Helium by too much too early can cause problems. In this instance we dropped the Helium by 15% but only raised the O2 by 10%, thus the inspired N2 percentage would have gone up by 5%. The result is that we can start to on-gas in any tissue that has a lower N2 tissue pressure than the inspired N2 pressure.

Should a tissue also have been at its N2 supersaturation limit then the result of the on-gassing can cause the supersaturation pressure to exceed its critical pressure ratio and a high risk of DCS would result. The better option would have been a 30/35 mix or to switch at a shallower depth where the Oxygen can take up the Helium drop. A 50/20 mix at 70 ft is commonly used by some divers.

For interest, if we waited the 2 minutes at the stop on back gas before we switch, the pressure in the 10 minute compartment would drop to the following.

P_{comp} = 3.03966 + [2.3591 – 3.03966] x [1 – 2 $^{-2/10}$]
P_{comp} = 3.03966 + [-0.68056] x [0.12945]
= 2.95156 atm Helium after 2 minute stop
This would lower the ratio for a 20% Helium to 2.95156 / 1.048485 = 2.8151 : 1
For a 30% Helium it would be 2.95156 / 1.57273 = 1.8767 : 1

Note that only one tissue compartment half time was used in the example, an algorithm will calculate the pressures for each compartment used in its calculations, and as mentioned before, if the half time values for the compartments between different computers differ, they will give different results. They cannot track what they do not use. ☺

Deep water blackout

Deep water blackout can occur due to a number of reasons, but is primarily thought to be due to Nitrogen narcosis in air diving, or from CO2 build up due to breathing a too dense gas at depth and not having the ability to properly ventilate the lungs or from working too hard, especially on high O2 mixes. Poor or malfunctioning gear may also add to the breathing resistance and divers under heavy narcosis may not notice the problem. CO2 build-up normally also increases respiration rate, however at sufficiently elevated levels it reduces respiration rate and may cause a hypoxic state to form.

Vertigo

Vertigo is a condition where the diver loses a sense of direction and position, and is brought on by a number situations. One possibility is for the ears to equalize out of balance with each other, either when descending or ascending. If one ear is equalized and the other not, the sensory mechanism of the diver may be temporarily affected and could result in vertigo. Due to the travel distance done by deep dives, with the need for possible stops on the ascent, the chances are higher for the ears not to equalize at the same time, a reverse block in one ear being a common problem.

Due to the depths reached in deeper diving, it is common that divers will descend and ascend without a visual reference, divers may also dive in conditions of limited visibility that will also create a scenario where descent and ascent are done without a reference. Possibilities exist where divers may be doing drift decompression and could hang for an hour or more in the water without any reference save maybe a liftbag line. The lack of visual reference can cause vertigo in the diver.

Vertigo symptoms can be from mildly annoying to incapacitating. The diver may experience extreme nausea with a feeling that everything is spinning. Tinnitus (ears ringing) may be experienced. The diver may not be able to focus on tasks at hand such as depth control and adhering to decompression schedules. From the nausea the diver may throw up, causing weakness and dehydration with the possibility of drowning.

In most cases vertigo can be prevented by descending and ascending slowly to give the ears time to equalize together, using a reference for descents and ascents (such as an anchor line or sloping bottom), closing the eyes for a moment should vertigo be experienced and holding on to something solid (such as a reference line, the bottom, or your buddy).

Increased risk for deep air diving

One might assume that it is logical that risk would increase the deeper one dives, however it is interesting to note that the risk for DCS increases around 5 to 10 times on deep air dives (dives below 150 ft on air) compared to Tri-Mix dives. This may be due to Helium diffusion being over conservatively calculated according to the Bühlmann tables, or that deep schedules are incorrect for deep air, or a number of other possibilities. Regardless of the actual reasons, deep air diving seems to be riskier than Helium mixed based gas diving to the same depth.

From analysis of French Navy diving the following is noted, the MN90 (MN = Marine Nationale) table for diving air to 60 m produces more incidences of DCS than the MN78 table for Tri-Mix diving to 80 m. The combined incidence for both tables is one in 30 000, however the incidence rate for the MN90 (deep air) table alone is around one in 3000.

From the gas properties of Helium it is thought that Helium needs a greater supersaturated partial pressure for bubbles to form than Nitrogen gas. However, from studies on 1400 rats on Helium and Nitrogen saturation it was found that Helium needed around 9 to 11% less supersaturated partial pressure to form bubbles. It was also seen that Helium and Nitrogen combined linearly to DCS risk compared to the safer component. Clearly gasses in the body behave differently than our understanding of them out of the body and Helium does not like to follow the ideal gas laws.

From animal experiments on high partial pressures of Oxygen (2 ata and higher) it was seen that N2 increased the risk of DCS with high O2 pressures. Goats were subjected to a PPO2 of 3.5 ata + PPN2 of 2 ata, this created a greater DCS incidence than if the PPO2 was 3.5 ata with PPN2 lowered or with 2 ata PPN2 and a lower PPO2. Later experiments found that O2 was around 88% as potent as N2 for serious DCS symptoms and around 38% as potent for fatal DCS. Thus at higher PPO2, Oxygen bends is a real concern and may explain partly why deep air diving has a higher DCS risk than Helium diving. However, at altitude Oxygen is far less potent than N2. In human tests of 477 dives it was found that an increase of 1 ata inspired O2 had the same DCS risk as an increase of 0.4ata inspired N2.

Effects of exercise in diving

Doing a quick morning jog or a gym session, then going for a nice dive where you carry your gear to the dive site just to follow it up with fighting waves to enter the water or swimming hard against a current in the dive, and lastly having to shlep your gear back home, just routine. However, how does that exercise affect you on and after the dive?

-Heavy exercise

A study into the effects of exercise was done by Dervay, J, MR Powell, BD Butler and CE Fife from NASA, called 'Effective lifetimes of tissue micronuclei generated by musculoskeletal stress' in Aviat. Space and Environ. Med., 68 (Suppl), A12. (1997).

By using Doppler devices in their study they concluded the following for non saturation dives: doing strenuous activity within four hours before a dive increases micronuclei, which increases venous gas emboli.

Anton Swanepoel

Musculoskeletal activity will increase tissue micronuclei and will persist for about two to five hours (proven in experiments), however it should be noted that it is not known exactly what will happen to these bubbles when they get compressed on a dive, although it is believed that they could play a role in DCS.

It is therefore advised to allow four hours before a dive after strenuous exercise and six hours after a dive before doing strenuous exercise. Do note that the term 'strenuous' can mean different things to different people and some may find just carrying their tanks back to their car strenuous, if so ask a friend to help.

It should be noted that for decompression diving, and especially saturation diving, these bubbles can play a larger part in DCS. On decompression dives and saturation dives things are a bit different. Due to exercise increasing blood flow, heavy exercise during diving, decompression stops and within hours after a dive should be avoided as these can pre-dispose you to DCS. The added blood flow may increase gas transport to and from the tissues too fast, overwhelming the body's ability to handle it and bubbles may form.

Tests done on divers to 60 ft for 60 minutes where they either rested or did exercise at the bottom showed an increase of 20% Nitrogen load for the divers that exercised. However, when divers were taken to 100 ft for 25 minutes and either exercised or not, an increase of 60% was seen in Nitrogen load for the divers that exercised. (Nitrogen load is the amount of Nitrogen they off-gassed after the dive.) In a study by Bühlmann and Schibli in 1972 it was found that divers that did work at depth needed around 20 to 44% more decompression than resting divers.

When doing exercise, Oxygen consumption increases and thus blood flow needs to increase as well. If considering that in many cases blood pressure and cardiac output is increased already by immersion in water, then doing heavy exercise can place the heart at considerable stress. If the person has high blood pressure this can be even more stressful to the heart, especially if the diver needs to handle heavy technical gear, as isometric work due to heavy lifting raises the arterial blood pressure that in turn increases the pressure load on the heart. Swimming with additional tanks causes drag that requires more work, this causes an increased flow demand from the heart, resulting in a volume load on the heart. Interestingly, a pressure work load is more demanding in terms of myocardial Oxygen consumption than an equivalent volume load, especially for people with high blood pressure.

Trivia: while it is known that doing a Valsalva maneuver causes blood pressure to increase, it is less known that sitting on the toilet and holding your breath while you force a bowel movement increases blood pressure dramatically and this has resulted in cardiac arrest and death in some people. Kinda shitty way to go out. ☺

-Light exercise

Light exercise before, during and after a dive however is a different matter. Light exercise here does not mean doing 20 push-ups, but rather the normal motion of kitting up your gear, doing a very gentle swim on the surface before dropping down, swimming slowly underwater, and doing gentle motions including swimming on deco stops. Since the blood flow is increased to the tissues slightly it helps in gas elimination on decompression stops and post dive. Before a dive it may help in reducing micronuclei and filtering out impurities found in the blood. If staying totally still on a deco stop (especially when breathing high PPO2, check section on high O2) the heart rate may slow down so much as to affect proper blood flow, affecting off-gassing. The time allotted for the deco stop may not be enough for the actual off-gassing rate.

Note that from tests it seems that light to mild continuous exercise during decompression does not increase bubble formation, where heavy or intermittent exercise does. Studies done by Jankowski have shown that light exercise during decompression reduces the amount of venous gas emboli.

-Exercise after diving

Since exercise increases perfusion, light exercise after a dive may help gas elimination and can be moderate, non-straining exercise, however avoid running, climbing ladders, and lifting weights or SCUBA tanks. If decompression stress is experienced (extremely tired and thirsty) then non strenuous movement (not exercise) is thought to be helpful in helping with gas elimination, sleeping should be avoided.

Hot shower or bath after a dive

After a dive you will still be off-gassing for hours to come, thus anything that alters blood circulation will affect off-gassing. When you take a hot bath or shower after a dive, your body will increase the blood flow to the skin in order to eliminate excess body heat, in addition to the arteries enlarging (vasodilation). The consequences of these changes are that blood is shunted away from muscles and other organs and directed to the skin, increasing skin perfusion while reducing perfusion to the muscles and other organs and can increase the risk for bubble formation and growth and DCS.

Anton Swanepoel

Pre-breathing before a deep dive

Due to the gas cost for deep dives, many divers are turning to rebreathers to conduct deep dives. One of the requirements for kitting up on a rebreather is to do a pre-breathe for around 5 minutes before entering the water. This is to check that all is ok with the unit, for it is better to pass out on the deck of a boat than underwater if there is a problem.

On the test, the unit is normally set to keep a constant PPO2 from around 0.4 ata to 0.8 ata. In effect the diver is breathing EAN40 to EAN80 on the surface. Most divers complete the procedure without knowing what they are actually doing to their bodies.

Since the diver is breathing a higher percentage of O2 and a lower percentage of N2, the diver is effectively flushing N2 out of the body, however more importantly the diver is also believed to reduce the size and number of micronuclei in the body. This in effect is seen as reducing your risk of DCS. The reduction in micronuclei is more effective if the diver does light exercise (like swimming on the surface to get out to a deeper point before dropping down), while breathing on the loop. Furthermore, note, the longer the pre-breathe the greater the effect.

Dental problems

Dental problems are not directly linked to deep diving, but to long durations in diving. Since deep diving has the diver normally stay in the water to decompress, these long durations can cause problems, where recreational divers may not see the same problems. However, a recreational diver or dive instructor who frequently dives may have the same problems.

Most divers are aware that loads of bacteria enter the mouth from the regulator mouthpiece - the mouthpiece gets wet when entering the water and bacteria may cling to it. In addition, many people wash their regulators with their wetsuits (which they may have urinated in) and then leave the regulator in the gear bag. Warm moist environment, a perfect home for bacteria to grow, waiting for your next bite. Suggestion is to wash the mouthpiece in fresh water on its own and disinfect before and after use with rubbing alcohol, a 10% bleach solution or a disinfectant bought from a dive shop.

However, this is not the extent of the problem nor the main problem. Few people realize the stresses the mouthpiece, regulator and CCR loop hoses put on the teeth and gums.

A short LP (low pressure) hose that constantly pulls the mouthpiece as you turn your head will increase the stress. The constant pull and push movement rocks the teeth back and forth, including side to side inside the gums (especially if a short mouthpiece is used that places all the stress on the front teeth). This movement can damage the teeth and gums and loosen the teeth. It is possible for bacteria to enter between the teeth and gums, creating infection (tooth abscess) that is painful, dangerous and expensive to fix. Untreated, a tooth abscess can spread to the ears, brain, and the rest of the body. Cases of heart attack and death have been recorded due to untreated tooth infections weeks after forming.

If your teeth, jaw or gums hurt after a dive, then you need to relook at the mouthpiece and regulator you are using. Possible solutions are to use a comfy bite mouthpiece that reaches further into the mouth and conforms to the shape of your teeth. Thus even pressure is exerted on all teeth and not just the front ones or ones that stand up higher than others.

A longer LP hose may help, as well as adding a swivel point at the regulator where the LP hose attaches to the regulator. This will create a more natural angle, it is true that it is an additional failure point and does restrict gas flow a bit, however you pick - dental problems and a sore jaw or possible o-ring failure and having to end a dive. The reduced flow rate is in any case not a problem if proper equipment for deep diving is used. Another possibility is looking at a smaller and lighter second stage regulator.

Few technical divers even think about the gear on their deco tanks. They are willing to splash out for top regulators for their back gas when doing OC dives, however they forget to get proper gear for their deco tanks that they may actually spend more time breathing from than their back gas regulators.

The loop from a CCR unit places loads of stress on the teeth and it is highly recommended to use a comfy bite mouthpiece here. Make sure the mouthpiece and the loop is properly aligned for you before you use it. Having one side more up will place most of the stress on one side of your mouth, teeth, gums, and jaw. Having the mouthpiece aligned pointing too far up or down will place additional stress either on the top or lower jaw and teeth.

Note for disinfection, you can use alcohol swabs, but that is expensive if you do many dives. Obtain a small spray bottle and fill it with rubbing alcohol. Give your mouthpieces a spray and wipe dry with paper towel or let it evaporate before diving. Alternatively use mouthwash in the spray bottle.

If you travel to a dive destination and rent regulators, then buy good mouthpieces and take them with, as rental regulators normally have very poor mouthpieces on. Ask the dive shop to attach your mouthpiece onto the regulator for the time of rental or do it yourself if you can.

A poor fitting mouthpiece may also cause temperomandibular joint syndrome due to clamping of teeth. This can cause pain in the jaw, neck, and face, and even headaches.

-Root canal and deep diving
Root canals are filled with a rubbery like material called gutta percha that flows under heat and pressure to be compressed into the canals. If the dentist filled the canal short, gas from the bloodstream may accumulate in the pocket at the bottom and may not be able to escape in time on the ascent, causing pain or even cracking of the tooth. Due to it being difficult to see the end of the canal, some dentists now use microscopes and fiber optic devices to see the end of the root canal.

If you need a root canal done, look for a specialist dentist who uses fiber optic and microscopes (especially for molars) as some research shows that nearly 30% of molars may have an extra canal that escapes detection visually. Note, if you dive with a temporary cap due to the tooth being prepared for a crown, then there can be an airspace in the tooth and the tooth can implode when diving. Either don't dive until the crown is done or ask your dentist to place a core in at the time of crown preparation.

Cardiac output changes
Tests were done where divers were given two schedules; one 66 ft (20 m) for 70 minutes and another 178 ft (54 m) for 20 minutes. The tests were first done in a wet chamber and repeated the following week in a dry chamber. It was noted that cardiac output and internal functions were reduced for up to two days after immersion in water but not for the dry chamber dives. Bubbles scores were also different and it was noted that decompression time was increased for the wet dives. This would make one wonder as to the long-term effect of diving on the heart and internal organs.

Pacemakers and deep diving
Most pacemakers will fail with increased pressure, with only a few models currently allowing some use underwater. These models have been proven safe to depths of around 100 ft (30 m) with a few deeper rated, however divers are advised to stay below 66 ft (20 m).

Note that only regurgitation pacemakers are generally thought to be OK for diving, but significant aortic or mitral valve stenosis (a narrowing in the opening of the aortic valve) precludes diving. Note also that models rated to at least 132 ft (40 m) are recommended and a complete medical with fitness check is advised.

Blood glucose drop

In tests done by Hamilton and coworkers, a drop in blood glucose level of around 33% was noted in divers breathing air at 132 ft (40 m) after 30 to 60 minutes.

Divers doing deep dives are thus urged to have a proper meal before a dive that is healthy and will sustain them for the duration of the dive. The glucose drop during a dive is also one of the reasons dive operators give candy or oranges to divers after a dive. Oranges and candy quickly allow blood sugar levels to rise after consuming. Glucose levels during a long dive can be supplemented with fruit juices and health bars underwater.

Gasses affecting bubble filtering

It was concluded from tests on dogs that halothane (a general anesthetic) interferes with the capacity of the lungs to filter air from the pulmonary circulation. Although it will be unlikely that you would have an operation requiring general anesthesia directly after a deep decompression dive, the question is what other gasses and chemicals interfere with the lungs' ability to filter bubbles that may be breathed before, during and after decompression? Deep divers working in habitats underwater or on surface supply air running directly off a compressor where the air intake of the compressor may pick up contaminants can affect the lungs' capacity to filter air and bubbles.

DCS in breath-hold divers

Native divers of Tuamotu Archipelago, Polynesia, have a malady called "Taravana", which is an acute decompression sickness due to rapid ascent from depths in excess of 165 ft (50 m) on breath-hold. The divers make around 40 to 60 short dives a day, each dive around 30 to 50 seconds bottom time, around 100 seconds total dive time, to depths in excess of 165 ft (50 m), to recover pearls.

Although Taravana symptoms are similar to those of DCS, for example paralysis, visual changes, hearing loss, dizziness and death, some symptoms are not. Hypoxia is proposed as the cause as divers struggle to get Oxygen into their lungs. Many divers end up with permanent brain and spinal cord injuries which could be seen as where breath-hold diving can possibly cause decompression sickness.

A book about Tarvana called 'Physiology of Breath-hold Diving and the Ama of Japan' edited by H. Rahn and T. Yokoyama was published in 1965 (publication number 1341 of the National Research Council, Washington D.C.).

Dr. Paulev, a Dane, took a submarine crew for training on submarine escape in Bergen, Norway in the 1960s. Freedivers would accompany the trainee submarine crew as they performed submarine escape ascents needed to qualify for naval submarine duty. The depth was 100 ft and Dr. Paulev did around 60 dives to depth with around 2 minutes bottom time each, followed by a surface interval of around 1-2 minutes. Dr. Paulev continued his dives and after around five hours of freediving he made his last dive, climbed out of the tank and collapsed as he walked away. He was promptly taken to a recompression facility and successfully treated.

As he was the medical officer on duty he wrote a report of the proceedings of the day, and an article for the Journal of Applied Physiology was later written. This was the first time DCS was recorded in freediving.

Dr. Paulev investigated the incidence further and concluded that the short surface interval was not enough to allow the Nitrogen to off-gas between dives. Dr. E. Lanphier did further studies on repeated breath-hold diving and calculated that if the surface interval equals the dive time then the Nitrogen loading would be equal to 50% of the depth for the duration of both the dive time and surface interval. For example, if a diver did a 140 ft dive for 2 minutes followed by a 2 minute surface interval, then the Nitrogen loading would be equal to a dive to 70 ft for 4 minutes (on rapid ascents the depth would be 65% of the bottom depth). A ratio of 2:1 for surface interval to bottom time reduces the depth to around 30% of the max breath-hold depth.

Breath-hold divers doing many repetitive dives over 100 ft are at great risk of developing DCS and so too breath-hold divers practicing for long durations (around three to five hours) even in shallower waters.

Narcosis from contaminants

Although this is not a problem for the average diver, it is still of interest to deep divers using dry decompression. It has been found that contaminants can cause a narcotic effect if brought into the dry chamber environment due to the increased pressures. Even small amounts of contaminates can cause serious problems for the occupants.

In 1997 two divers in a saturation bell became increasingly narcotic after the return of a diver from a contaminated site. The divers realized something was wrong at a stage when they were still functioning and flushed the diving bell. This prompted research into sensors to warn occupants of potential narcotic or toxic gases.

Although saturation diving bells are far safer now and isolation protocols stricter, there is a concern for deep divers (especially cave divers) that set up their own dry chambers and deep stop station from various materials underwater. The open home-made chambers are easily contaminated from not only the surroundings but also the diver's gear and water or residue on the diver's gear.

Cave divers who also enter dry submerged areas need to take note of the possibility of contaminated gas (not to mention low O2), these contaminants can come from the local environment such as water, dirt, rock and possible rotting fish or plants.

Altitude and deep diving

Although altitude diving is also done by recreational divers, it has an increased effect on the technical diver.

At altitude the ambient pressure that the diver will experience on surfacing is less than at sea level. Thus, a diver will need to surface with a lower surpersaturation in the tissues to prevent DCS. If planned for it is not a problem for the tech diver, however what is a problem is the reduced partial pressure of O2 that the diver will breathe upon surfacing. During decompression the diver will most likely use a gas with a higher O2 content than air to accelerate decompression. When the diver breathes the ambient air upon surfacing the PPO2 will drastically drop and in most cases will be hypoxic (lower than 0.21 ata). The result is that lung shunting will drastically increase that could cause bubbles to bypass the lungs.

An additional problem is that divers may be short of breath for some time due to the lower O2 pressure, and the diver may pass out on the surface or immediately after a dive, especially if the diver exits the water with heavy dive gear.

Anton Swanepoel

Claustrophobia

Although it is unlikely that people suffering from claustrophobia (afraid of being in a tight small space) will practice deep diving, it has been noted that some subjects that were isolated from environment stimuli (possibly bell diving or diving in very low visibility) started experiencing hallucinations after two to three hours. Deep air subjects are more at risk due to narcosis and incidences have been noted of delirium after 20 minutes at 158 ft (48 m).

Dehydration

When diving on open circuit, a diver loses water due to the air the diver breathes being dryer than normal air on the surface. For the CCR diver, this is not normally a concern as the lost water vapor stays in the loop and humidifies the dry air that is in the loop so that further water loss is limited, in addition to the CCR diver using less gas on the dive than OC. On long OC dives, especially on long decompression dives, the water loss can be great and divers may need to replenish fluids underwater.

Squeeze packets of fruit juice consumed with a straw work well underwater, although normal sports drink bottles can be consumed underwater as well with a little bit of practice. Sports drink bottles with a lid that can seal by pushing a small ring back with your tongue is the best. Some divers use camel packs that have a bite valve (the same as is used by outdoor hikers and motorcycle riders).

For interest, a diver loses around 0.043 ml of water per liter of air breathed. Thus for a standard 80 cu ft (11.1 free liter) tank (2275.5 L at 205 bar) the diver will lose around 98 ml of water. This may seem small, and may be so for recreational diving if the diver is well hydrated, however the diver will lose additional water due to sweating and urination in the dive that can become a problem, especially if the diver does multiple dives and does not hydrate after the dive.

For technical divers, the water loss may become a problem. Take a dive where the diver uses 160 cu ft bottom gas and needs three slings with a usage of 63 cu ft each to complete the dive. That is 349 cu ft of gas, the diver will lose around 428 ml of water through ventilation alone. Coupled with sweating and urination the diver can lose a great deal that will not only increase the diver's DCS risk, but also the diver's performance, reasoning and memory in the dive.

If you lose 2½% of your body weight in water you lose 25% of your performance. Remember the body loses around 1.5 to 3 L of water per day normally that needs to be replaced.

The loss through breathing dry air and immersion effect causing urination will increase this amount. From these numbers it is clear that many people live in a constant state of partial dehydration. Read the book "You are not sick, you are thirsty" from F. Batmanghelidj, for more information.

Hypothermia

Due to most deep dives being conducted in cold water, hypothermia is a reality for many technical divers. Many divers use a drysuit to protect them from the cold. However, even in warmer waters, becoming cold is still a concern due to the length of most of the dives and due to wetsuit compression at depth causing loss in thermal protection. Water conducts heat away around 25 times faster than air and as such a diver will get cold faster in the same temperature of water than had the person been in air. A person can thus tolerate a lower air temperature without getting cold than the same water temperature as the water will conduct heat away faster than the body can generate it.

Note that hypothermia is not skin temperature, but internal body temperature and a person can become hypothermic without feeling cold.

Another way divers lose heat that is not often thought of is through ventilation. The air we breathe on land has water vapor in, however the air we breathe underwater is dry and the body humidifies the air. In the process water is lost (see dehydration section). In order to vaporize the water, body heat is needed. It is thought that around 15% of the heat loss underwater is due to ventilation. Since the body heats the inhaled gas to body temperature, exhaled gas is around 98.6 °F (37 °C) and the body saturates this with water vapor, around 47 mmHG vapor pressure. The body needs around 0.58 Kcal/g to vaporize water, thus will use around 0.025 kilocalories per liter of gas consumed for vaporization.

A diver who uses 27 L/minute (1620 L/hour) will lose 40.40 Kcal/hr due to vaporization. Note, a standard 80 cu ft tank holds around 2275.5 L of free gas, and 1620 L gas usage is normal for an hour dive at recreational depths.

Heat is additionally lost due to the body needing to heat the inspired gas. Due to the gas being in a cylinder open to the elements, the inspired gas temperature is normally the same or very close to ambient temperature. Heat loss due to gas warming is 0.241 cal/g/°C (Helium loss is 1.25872 cal/g/°C) difference between inspired gas temperature and internal body temperature 37 °C.

Anton Swanepoel

Air at 37 °C weighs 1.138 g/liter (Helium weighs 0.157g/liter at 37 °C). If the temperature difference is 22 °C, taking the same amount of gas as from before (1620 L/hour) then 9.77 Kcal/hr will be lost. (1620L * 1.138 g/L = 1843.56 g * 0.241 cal/°C = 444.29796 cal * 22 °C = 9774.55 cal/hr or 9.77 Kcal/hr).

With increased pressures the gas becomes denser and heavier, thus heat loss will increase the denser the gas is. At 330 ft (100 m) the heat loss will be 9.77 Kcal * 11 = 107.47 Kcal/hr only to heat the gas with a total of 185.39 Kcal/hr heat loss when taking into account humidifying the gas.

To this needs to be added heat loss due to convection and radiation, however this value will differ a lot between divers and is due to their exposure protection, subcutaneous fat layer, shell thickness, cold water adaption, skin temperature, and water movement over the body. Note should be taken that people with a higher fat layer are able to reduce heat loss in cold water (a reduction from 33 to 2.2 Kcal/m²/°C/hr in some cases was recorded). Lean individuals with little subcutaneous fat are not able to reduce heat loss as much as people with a higher fat layer. Heat loss is increased the greater the difference is between skin temperature and ambient temperature.

Note that CCR users do not lose heat as OC divers do due to the chemical reaction with the scrubber and CO2. In general every liter of air exhaled under normal diving conditions contains around 1/400 g CO2 and will produce around 0.065 Kcal of heat. For the same ventilation rate (27 L/minute) the gas volume of 1620 L will then produce 105.3 Kcal/hr of heat. In cold water this greatly helps the diver to stay warmer, however in warm water the result may be that the diver can easily overheat on a long dive, especially if the diver exerts himself and CO2 production rises. Additionally in CCR divers, heat loss through vaporization is reduced drastically due to water and heat being produced in the chemical reaction between CO2 and the scrubber material.

Alcohol consumption causes vasodilatation that increases heat loss, in addition to alcohol inactivating nerve centers and the hypothalamic (an almond sized portion of the brain that controls body temperature, hunger, thirst, fatigue, sleep, and circadian cycles). Thus, alcohol consumption before a dive or diving while being hungover is not a good idea.

-Signs of hypothermia

As the internal temperature of the body decreases from the normal 98.6 °F (37 °C), the body responds in different ways. The first signs of hypothermia are increased use of Oxygen and ventilation to cope with the increased metabolic activity for heat production.

Shivering occurs to help with muscle activity and heat production (note that muscles can increase heat production without increased activity, and around 45% of heat production is from extramuscular activity), vasoconstriction occurs to try and limit blood flow to the extremities and heat generation rate is increased by increasing metabolic rate.

At 93.2 °F (34 °C), amnesia, dysarthria (from 'dys' meaning 'having a problem with' and 'arthr' meaning 'articulating', difficulty speaking) and loss of conscious perception is found in addition to the heart rate dropping around 50 beats/minute. At 86 °F (30 °C) anesthesia is observed and shivering ceases with the muscles becoming rigid for around 50 minutes where the muscles relax. At 80.6 °F (27 °C) cessation of voluntary movement is found. At 75.2 °F (24 °C) respiration stops.

Hypothermia can be treated by immersing the body in 104 to 122 °F (40 to 50 °C) water for around 10 minutes to rewarm the body while giving warm fluids to drink, however note that if the stage of muscle relaxation is reached, then hypothermia may be irreversible at this point.

Calorie needs and deep diving

From the section on dehydration and hypothermia one can see that the body needs more energy when diving than on the surface. In general a diver on open circuit needs around 450 to 500 Kcal /hr, and a fully closed rebreather diver around 400 to 450 Kcal/hr under the same conditions, taking that a body at rest on the surface needs around 70 Kcal/hr, this is a big increase. A fit diver can maintain around 700 Kcal/hr production for around 10 to 12 hours where others struggle to meet the required demand, which shows why some people easily get cold and tired on a dive, especially if more than moderate swimming is needed. A diver can thus easily use up 1500 Kcal for a three-hour decompression dive and supplemental energy intake in a liquid form (liquid squeeze container meal replacements) is recommended.

On observing breath-hold fisherman in competition that dove to around 83 to 100 ft (25 to 30 m) for up to six hours a day for two days, it was noted that they lost up to 10 kg during the competition.

Not eating before a dive can thus easily cause a diver to become tired, light headed, cold, experience headaches, have difficulty reasoning and solving problems, in addition to remembering details.

Protein loss during a dive

From studies done by various groups and people including Kovacs and Gabor, it was seen that proteinuria (loss of protein through the urine) occurs when swimming in cold water and is thought to be due to a change in kidney function due to the cold and pressure exerted on it (some exposure suits have added warmth protection in the kidney area). Thus, it is suggested that divers increase their protein intake, especially when diving in cold water (protein bars and shakes are a good option). If protein is not replaced, muscle loss has been noted in divers diving in cold waters.

However, note that large meals should not be eaten before a dive, especially if they contain hard to digest foodstuff such as fats, and the dive is in cold water. Easy to digest foods such as fruits, salads, protein bars, protein shakes and meal replacements should be eaten before a dive as the circulatory reflexes involved in digestion interfere with the diencephalic adaption response when the body is immersed in cold water. Further note that lighter foods such as salads and fruits increase the body's metabolic rate, where heavy foods such as fries and burgers slow down the body's metabolic rate and heat production, not to mention sludging of the blood.

Salt effect on the skin

The salt crystals in minute form that cling to the skin (even when swimming in a wetsuit) cause stimula to the sensory nerve endings that have a sympathetic neurotonic (strengthens) and regulating effect on the pituitary and the thyroid. This helps to offset hypophysial secretion due to a thermal response.

Medication and deep diving

Although many medications are contraindicated even for recreational diving, any diver using any medication while deep diving should carefully consider the effects that the medication can have before making the dive. On deeper dives the Oxygen partial pressure and exposure will normally far exceed those found in recreational diving and the drug may react far differently than expected. To this can be added the half life of the drug - in elevated partial pressure of Oxygen the drug may work better (creating a stronger reaction that could be unpleasant), in addition to lasting a shorter time. Thus, the drug's effect may wear off before the end of the dive, with possible unpleasant consequences.

Chapter 9

Women and deep diving

This chapter deals with the unique problems women face when diving, especially deep diving as it normally entails longer dives, and looks at the risk for women in deep diving especially when using oral or injection contraceptives, during pregnancy and the menstrual cycle.

Diving while pregnant

Although the current suggestion is not to dive while pregnant due to little currently being known about the developing fetus and pressure, deep or decompression diving is highly ill advised while pregnant.

Studies done by Betts found that diving below 100 ft (30 m) during the first trimester had a rate of around 16% abnormality in the fetus from the women tested. In another test of women diving while pregnant on shallower depths there were no abnormalities in the fetus. Studies done on pregnant sheep with dives that resulted in decompression sickness in late pregnancy had increased fetal morbidity and mortality. Dives that had no decompression sickness had no effect on the fetus. In studies it was also found that hyperbaric Oxygen treatment may be toxic to the fetus.

The main problem in deep diving and decompression is that the fetus and unborn child have no developed lungs. The lungs are bypassed due to the PFO (hole in the heart, known as a foramen ovale in a fetus), all the Oxygen the fetus needs is supplied by the mother's blood due to the fetus lungs not yet functioning. Oxygenated blood flowing into the fetal heart does not flow out to the lungs, but flows through the fetus body and then returns to the fetal heart where it exits via the umbilical vein into the mother's bloodstream. Thus should any bubbles be present in the mother's blood then it can be passed directly to an unprotected fetus brain and body.

For interest, during birth the blood vessels in the umbilical cord constrict and cut off all flow to the placenta, resulting in a rapid drop in blood O2 levels in the newborn while CO2 rises. Like a butterfly out of a cocoon, the newborn's chest expands after being constricted by the birth canal, causing the lungs to expand with the chest. This expansion causes air to be drawn into the lungs and the newborn takes in its first breath while at the same time the forum ovale closes (in most people). With the closure of the forum ovale blood now flows to the lungs where they are now used for the first time. A cry from the newborn is a sign that the lungs and pulmonary circuit are working and that the newborn is breathing properly.

Anton Swanepoel

Blood shunting in the lungs is a reality in diving and when decompressing from a decompression dive divers normally use higher pressures of Oxygen to accelerate decompression. This elevated pressure of Oxygen may cause harm to the fetus depending on the pressure used and time spent at elevated pressures. For more information on lung blood shunting see 'Deep and Safety Stops, including Ascent Speed and Gradient Factors'.
http://www.antonswanepoelbooks.com/deepstops.php

It was also shown in studies on sheep that the fetus may have bubbles while the mother shows no signs of decompression sickness or bubbles. Also note that the blood complement activation trigger point for bubbles in the system may differ for the fetus than in the mother. See above mentioned book for more details on blood protein complement activation due to bubbles. Deep and decompression diving increase the risk of bubble formation and DCS.

Another concern when diving while pregnant is morning sickness that can induce gastro-oesophageal reflux, possibly resulting in vomiting. If the diver cannot make it to the surface in time, she may vomit underwater which can cause loss of buoyancy or possibly drowning.

-DCS treatment while pregnant

Although there is no evidence currently that diving while pregnant increases DCS risk to the mother, if the mother does get DCS then the treatment may place the fetus at risk. Standard treatment for DCS is hyperbaric Oxygen where Oxygen is given at elevated pressures. However, in the fetus arterial blood flow decreases dramatically when the Oxygen tension in the pulmonary circulation increases due to the fetal pulmonary bed being sensitive to Oxygen tension. The response is vasodilatation with raised Oxygen tension. There is consequently a blood flow shift from the fetus to the mother. Although the shift will reverse when the Oxygen tension returns to normal, it is however unknown if the shift has any long term damage to the fetus.

-Marine poison and pregnancy

Note should be taken that certain marine poison may be toxic to the fetus and can have unknown effects on the fetus, as can specific antitoxins. Some like a lionfish sting can be life threatening to the fetus even if it does not pose a serious risk to the mother. (Note lionfish and other stings can be life threatening to the mother, a fellow dive instructor of the author was hospitalized on morphine after a lionfish sting).

Diving while menstruating

When talking about menstruating and diving risk, most people think blood and sharks, however in most cases this is not a problem. Had it been the only thing women had to contend with when menstruating, life would be a lot simpler.

A study of all the reports of women who developed altitude DCS found that all the women were in their first 14 days of their menstrual cycle. This has been supported by later studies showing an inverse correlation between the number of days since the last menstrual period and the incidence of altitude DCS. The exact reason for this is not known, however due to the menstrual cycle changing hormones in the body, it may change the blood protein complement activation trigger to foreign objects in the blood in order to protect the body. Thus the complement activation point may be more sensitive and trigger on a smaller size and amount of bubbles in the blood than would normally not have caused problems.

Women face another problem when menstruating, pain. Although most women go through their monthly cycle reasonably OK (maybe a few mood swings and broken plates ☺), other women have lots of pain with it. The pain can be so severe to be incapacitating and can last for several days. This can be even worse if the woman does not know when exactly her cycle will start, either because not all women follow an exact cycle or the cycle sometimes shifts by a few days due to a number of influences. The main problem is that if pain starts underwater for a female recreational diver, she may surface albeit in pain. A female deep diver may still need to do hours of painful decompression, and should the period pains cause incapacitation, then it can cause a serious risk underwater. In this case deep or decompression diving is not advised when nearing the start of menstruation.

-Premenstrual Syndrome (PMS) and deep diving

PMS is associated with hormonal changes resulting in a range of symptoms normally around a week before menses (the period). As with menstruation, some women have it lucky while others have severe symptoms that can include personality changes and problems with task loading, and symptoms seem to worsen as the diver ages due to a wider range of estrogen swings. For deep diving the diver may become moody, in addition to possibly making incorrect decisions, especially in an emergency, with the risk increasing the more severe the PMS symptoms are. Hormone replacements have been noted to decrease PMS symptoms.

Anton Swanepoel

Oral and injection contraceptives

Although contraceptive medication is normally safe while diving, woman wanting to do decompression or deep diving would be advised to first note the chemicals in the drug they are taking and consult a doctor or Divers Alert Network before diving. Certain drugs react differently under elevated pressures of Oxygen and it has been speculated that the haematological effects of the early contraceptive pill could increase susceptibility to DCS due to the pill encouraging microsludging of the blood peripherally. Some pills are known to be associated with an increased risk of thromboembolism due to them accelerating blood clotting and increasing platelet aggregation.

Certain injections or once a month pills may also be very strong and their effect directly after taking can induce tiredness, memory loss and inability to concentrate, especially under elevated pressures of Oxygen. If contraceptive medication does cause problems after taking it, then deep diving should be avoided until the symptoms disappear, and alternative medication or other contraceptive ways should be sought.

Breast Implants

When women with breast implants first started diving, a lot of myths surfaced where implants were supposed to have broken or exploded. This has been seen not to be true and women should have no fear doing normal recreational dives with implants. From a study by Vann on implants (silicone, saline and silicone/saline filled) in a hyperbaric chamber, it was found that there was an increase in the size of the implants and bubbles did form in the implant. It was also found that saline implants absorbed less Nitrogen than silicone implants, while silicon implants enlarge the most and have the most bubbles.

When the implants were exposed to high altitude after a dive to simulate flying after diving, significant volume changes occurred. However, it was not enough to cause a rupture and the bubbles resolved over time. From the pressure changes the implants were seen to handle in the tests, the thought is that there should be no problem for women divers with implants so long as correct decompression protocols are followed. This is due to the implants being able to handle a larger supersaturation level than what would cause DCS symptoms.

Breast Feeding

Women nursing may wonder if bubbles can form in the breast milk, especially on deep dives and if it can harm infants. From tests it was found that bubbles do not seem to form in breast milk and if it did it would not pose a problem to the infant as it is not entering the blood stream but the gastrointestinal tract. At worst the infant may just get a nice milkshake. ☺

What can be more of a problem in deep and long dives is breast engorgement (due to a buildup of milk) that can become uncomfortable, especially with tight dive gear and heavy straps or gear over the chest.

A larger concern however is the possibility of marine pathogens being transferred from the mother's nipples to the infant that can result in stubborn infectious diarrhea. This is actually a possibility for all mothers entering the ocean or any water (especially swimming pools) and breast feeding, and mothers are urged not to breast feed the infant until a shower or bath has been taken and the nipple cleaned (possibly with an alcohol swab). An additional problem is that bacteria can also enter exposed nipple ducts or skin breaks, causing a severe mastitis (inflammation of breast tissue).

Women breastfeeding and deep diving should also be aware of the possibility of dehydration and exhaustion that can cause a decrease in milk production.

Overheating

Women have fewer sweat glands than men, in addition to starting to sweat later than men, allowing a higher core temperature before sweating begins, which combined with women's thicker shell (nope that has nothing to do with being hard headed or stubborn. ☺) allows them to conserve heat. The 'shell' is the thickness between the skin and the circulation level and functions as an insulatory mechanism and vasoconstriction thickens the shell. Women have more subcutaneous (under the skin) fat than men resulting in a greater insulation against heat loss. However, it also makes them susceptible to overheating when sitting in the sun fully kitted up.

Hypothermia

Although women can conserve heat better than men, women do have problems when they get cold as they cannot recover heat as easily as men due to their lower basal metabolic rate. Women who constantly face cold conditions are however able to adapt better than men, as seen from the Korean Ama (female freedivers) that dive in water as low as 50 °F (10 °C).

It was found that the women had a higher basal metabolic rate to compensate for heat loss. Women are also able to constrict their blood vessels (vasoconstriction) more than men to conserve body heat.

Decompression

The following is true for the difference between any two people with different fat and muscle content, however, in general women have more body fat than men, with men also having more muscle than women. NASA has done many years of research for their space programs to eliminate decompression sickness for astronauts. What they found was that the amount of N2 in the fat tissues of women is around double that in men, while the amount of N2 in lean tissues of men is slightly greater than in women.

Thus during the start of decompression and on ascent, a large amount of N2 is eliminated from a well-perfused lean tissue in men, with a smaller amount of N2 coming from a poorly perfused fat tissue. In women N2 is also released initially from a well-perfused lean tissue, however the amount will be less than in men and off-gassing quantity per minute will fall faster in men.

Since women have a larger reservoir of N2 than men coming from fat, it is thought that a longer end decompression is needed to eliminate the slow off-gassing tissue. Men are then seen to in general have a faster peak in off-gassing on initial decompression that stays high longer than in women, where women have a shorter initial off-gassing curve but have a longer tail off-gassing curve. Thus it would seem that men are more sensitive for faster ascents and missing first stops, and women are more sensitive for omitting the last deco stops, in a perfect world. Oops, we live on earth. ☺ Note that no two people have identical N2 uptake and elimination kinetics, thus the above point is highly academic when comparing men and women in general, but does make for an interesting after-dive conversation piece.

Chapter 10

Men and deep diving

This chapter deals with the physiological problems men face while diving. And nope **ego** is not a physiologic problem although it may well be a problem in diving accidents. ☺

Heat loss

Although very small women radiate more heat compared to large men due to a larger surface area to mass ratio, women do compensate for this through heat preserving mechanisms. Extensive research by military and private sector laboratories on heat loss found no comparative threat to woman's core temperature, even on extended and extreme cold exposure. Men however do not fare so well due to a number of disadvantages.

Men have a lesser vasoconstrictor response to cold than women, resulting in a higher blood flow in their shell, resulting in less insulation and faster heat loss and also higher skin temperatures than women. The heat loss is greater the greater the difference is between skin temperature and water temperature, called a high shell to environment gradient. Men's genitals are also at risk the same as fingers, however genitals carry a high blood flow with little protection and can result in 'Frostbite Shorts' (a documented medical malady). This is the reason why pearl fishing in Japan is reserved for women, as the cold is believed to cause sterility in men.

High calorie requirement

Due to the high heat loss, men have to compensate with increased metabolic effort, requiring more calories. For long, especially cold dives men need to make sure they have a proper meal before the dive and possibly supplement calorie intake with protein bars and sports drinks underwater.

Eating underwater is not that difficult, especially when diving on open circuit. Bigger men, especially muscular men need more calories to maintain their body weight and temperature (muscle burns more calories than fat). If the diver did not take in enough calories before the dive, tiredness may result (especially when swimming with additional tanks against a current).

Divers may also become irritated and can make judgment errors, especially in emergencies. For divers with health conditions such as low blood sugar, low blood pressure or other problems special note should be taken to eat meals when deep diving (blood glucose drops with deep diving, see Blood glucose drop).

Hypoglycemia from compressed air breathing is thought to be due to the high pressure of Oxygen in the mix under pressure. Barthelemy noted a 16% decrease in erythrocyte potassium in blood serum after 30 minutes in divers at 100 ft (30 m) that continued to decrease slightly even after decompression (30 minutes). It should also be noted that the subjects tested were in a chamber at rest, exercising at depth will further deplete glucose levels.

It was also noted that interstellar potassium, total blood lipids and blood calcium levels dropped during the dives tested above. It was noted that there were only small variations in the amount of blood glucose and minerals drop between subjects at rest or working and subjects in dry chambers or immersed in water. Thus hyperbaric glycemia seems to be a response to breathing air under pressure and is thought to be a change in the liver and metabolic rate due to changes in blood flow under pressure. Levels returned slowly after a dive and in some cases took days to return to normal.

Overheating

Large men, especially muscular men, are more likely to overheat than women due to men generating more heat than women, in addition to dissipating heat less efficiently in hot weather. Men normally have a smaller surface area to mass ratio that limits the amount of heat they can radiate away, in addition to men's high skin temperature creating a smaller shell to environment gradient in hot weather, impeding heat loss.

Dehydration

Men begin sweating at a lower temperature than woman and sweat more than women, in addition men are wasteful sweaters in that they sweat more than what can be evaporated. It is not the amount of sweat you make that causes body heat loss, but the amount that evaporates, drawing heat away with it. Any additional sweat that cannot evaporate does not add any advantage. The result is that men lose more body fluids than women when comparing body size. Men also need more water than women due to their higher metabolic rate and larger size, putting them at a higher risk of dehydration, in addition to men possibly losing more electrolytes than women that on a long dive can cause electrolyte imbalance, especially if the person does not take in sufficient amounts of minerals and salt in his daily intake.

Fertility

Due to men's productive organs not being protected as well as women's, both cold and hot water affects male fertility. Thermal influence to male fertility has been known for centuries and is thought to be one of the reasons Scotsmen invented kilts. Some studies on pearl divers of the South Seas found that the men's fertility lowered after cold water excursions.

Air consumption

Due to men's larger size, higher metabolic rate, higher body heat and larger muscle mass, men need more Oxygen to sustain them and as a result have larger lungs, resulting in more air taken in with every breath. This results in men using more air than women in general with two to three times higher air consumptions normal. Although women can waste air as well due to incorrect breathing, men will waste a larger amount than women with incorrect breathing (shallow and fast). Air consumption is additionally increased due to men's normal bad body posture in the water, especially large men as men normally carry more of their fat on their upper bodies, making their legs leaner and heavier. This causes the legs to sink and increase drag in the water. Men also have a threefold higher back injury rate over women due to their larger upper body, and with heavy tech gear it is a big concern.

Chapter 11

Supplements for deep diving

There are many supplements on the market today and many books and articles can be found on the subject of supplements, thus this section is an overview of some of the supplements that can be considered for deep diving without making a pill munching addict out of you.

Note, always consult with a professional dietitian, doctor, pharmacist or a personal trainer before taking any supplements.

Adding multivitamins into your diet will help your body stay in top condition to fight off intruders. Vitamin C is in great need and can be supplemented with pills, or from natural fruits and vegetables. Zinc helps fight infections and needs to be in your supplement. Onions and garlic, being from the same family, are great fighters of infection and help keep your body clean. Echinacea will boost your immune system, get one that includes Goldenseal.

Highly processed food should be avoided, not just for their empty calories and creating an extra butt on you, but for the high level of sugar and sugar related products found in it. Sugar taxes the body's defense system, weakening it and allowing bacteria to get a foothold easier. Remember to drink plenty of water before and after a dive, including if possible during long dives.

Eat plenty of fresh fruit and vegetables, but do include seeds, nuts and possibly meat (in moderation) in your diet to obtain protein. Fish and chicken are good options, but if you like an occasional red meat meal it is ok.

Ginkgo

Some studies have found a standardized ginkgo extract to be beneficial for a wide variety of conditions associated with aging, including tinnitus, vertigo, memory loss, concentration problems, confusion, depression, anxiety, dizziness, headache, and poor circulation. Although some studies have found no benefit to tinnitus sufferers, there is basically no side effects and memory improvement has been shown in studies. Ginkgo works slowly, and it may take several weeks or even months before experiencing any relief. Suggest use Ginkgo with Goldenseal.

Diet

Arteriosclerosis (high blood pressure) is mostly a result of poor diet. Things to minimize or avoid are animal protein (especially red meat), refined flours and sugars, and processed foods which constrict the arteries and stress the body. Since anything that constricts the arteries can increase DCS risk, its intake should be avoided or limited, especially just before or after a long decompression dive.

Vitamin B complex

Vitamin B (especially B12, B6, B2, B1, B3 (Niacin) and B5 (pantothenic acid)) has been shown to improve concentration and coping with stress, your brain uses a large amount of resources when trying to concentrate on keeping you alive underwater, replenish your resources. These vitamins form part of a combination of vitamins that is essential for metabolism, food processing and energy production.

Vitamin B12 deficiency is a possible cause of tinnitus and is often found in high stress and high noise working environments. Vitamin B12 can be found in yeast, oysters, eggs, milk and milk products, fish, poultry, and lamb.

Vitamin B3 (Niacin) is contained in all the cells of the body with a surplus supply stored in the liver, Niacin is crucial for human health as without it metabolism is seriously affected. Try whole-grain products, bananas, most fruits and vegetables, eggs, dairy products, chicken, tuna and salmon, mushrooms, liver, coffee, asparagus, halibut and venison.

Vitamin A

Vitamin A deficiency can cause inner-ear problems such as ear tinnitus and ear infections since it is important for the membranes in the ear. With long dives ear infection is a large concern. Try oily fish, dark green leafy vegetables, blueberries, yellow vegetables, carrots, yams, oranges, apricots and cantaloupe.

Vitamin E

Vitamin E helps to strengthen the immune system and fight illnesses while also improving oxygen supply to the cells. Since your body is under a lot of stress while underwater, give it the best you can to defend itself. Vitamin E also helps lower DCS risk. Try whole-grain products, dried beans, green leafy vegetables, fish, and eggs. Note that Vitamin E is a water soluble vitamin and excess amounts are stored in the body, thus do not take more than 1000 units a day. Taking more can lead to diarrhea and dizziness.

Vitamin C

Vitamin C helps to defend the body from infections and bacteria. Many people think that sea water is clean, however there are loads of bacteria in the water that can cause infections. Cuts and scrapes are common in diving and more so in technical diving. Do not exceed a dose of more than 1000 mg per day.

Zinc

Zinc deficiency has been linked to tinnitus and ear infections, and zinc supplements have been shown to reduce tinnitus in people suffering from both tinnitus and hearing loss. Note, take no more than 80 mg daily. Try oysters, whole-grain cereals, beans, nuts, eggs, fish, spinach (the best), papaya, collards, brussel sprouts, cucumbers, string beans, endive, cowpeas, prunes and asparagus. Note Zinc is slow acting and it may take up to eight months to see results.

Protein bars

Diving causes protein loss that needs to be replaced. Protein is also good for fuel without slowing your circulation system down like fat, nor spiking your insulin levels like sugars. Most protein bars can be consumed under water with a little practice. Make sure you read the ingredients on the packet as many so called health bars are nothing more than candy bars loaded with junk.

A note on sports supplements

Some divers use energy drinks (such as Red Bull) and body building or extreme sports drinks while diving. This may be in the belief that it helps them for energy on long dives or to cope with a hangover from the previous night's party.

Divers should however realize that many of these drinks can cause heart palpitations and hypertension, especially those marketed towards body builders. With the additional load your heart is under when diving, it does not need extra stimulants pushing it along. Many of the drinks also contain high amounts of caffeine and sugar, not a good combination when diving.

End note

A good make of a one a day multi vitamin supplement in addition to a multi complex B supplement will in most cases be sufficient. You require a lot from your body, give some back.

Chapter 12

Gear consideration

Due to the increased pressure on deeper dives, gear choice becomes far more critical and important compared to shallower dives.

Depth

One of the biggest problems is pressure, gear (especially flashlights, dive computers and cameras) may catastrophically fail (implode or crush), crack, non catastrophically fail (leak and malfunction), or permanently deform.

It is important to read the manufacturers' depth rating for all gear that you intend to purchase, and verify that they can operate at the depths you intend to dive to.

Time

Due to the nature of decompression diving normally being longer dives compared to recreational dives, time becomes a factory for gear selection.

As you will be in the water longer, you need to get adequate thermal protection to guard against becoming cold or worse hypothermic. On a normal dive you may just ascend to the surface and end the dive when you become cold, however this is not normally the case in decompression diving as you may still have a long decompression schedule ahead of you.

Proper gear fit becomes very important on these long dives. A poor fitting mask that rubs you or leaks slightly may be tolerated on a short shallow dive, but on long deep dives it can be from very uncomfortable to dangerous. This goes for fins and all other gear such as booties, wetsuits, drysuits and BCDs.

A factor sometimes overlooked is flashlight burn time. A dive light with a 70 or 90 minute burn time may be ample for a shallow short recreational dive, but on long technical dives, often approaching and exceeding two hours, you will need more burn time.

BCD and regulators

Due to the added gear and possibly tanks that you will be using on the dive, it is not uncommon to be overweight at the beginning of the dive. You need a BCD that has an adequate lift capacity to deal with the additional weight; in most cases you may need a double bladder BCD, one for backup. Note that the deeper you go, the slower your BCD inflates, especially true for lower cost models.

It has occurred that divers heavily weighted doing fast descents, waiting till the last moment to inflate the BCD, could not stop. The BCD inflator was not able to provide gas and inflate the BCD compared to the speed of descent. The gas to create lift that was added to the BCD was ineffective due to the BCD being compressed from the additional pressure as the diver kept on going deeper. Choose high-performance equipment and keep in control of your descent.

Although Helium in diving mixtures reduces the gas density of the breathing gas, it may still be more than surface air density when breathed at depth. Some lower cost second stage models are not designed to be used deeper than 100 ft (30 m) and some even as shallow as 60 ft (18 m). Using these regulators at depth can cause from high breathing resistance and work of breathing to inability to get sufficient gas.

The total gas volume able to be delivered from the regulator first stage also needs to be checked, it needs to be able to provide the gas requirements of two divers sharing gas and inflating their BCDs at the same time. Note that in an emergency, divers in panic can easily double their breathing rate.

From tests done to determine the effects of 'J' valve levers as a reserve for use on offshore deep diving an interesting observation was made. It was noted that modern balanced regulators could function without much noticeable increase in breathing resistance when the tank pressure was near its critical pressure and that some breathed normally and then suddenly cut off air supply even mid breath. Older regulators would slowly become harder to breathe from but modern regulators may be so balanced that they function well at even very low tank pressures and not always give advance warning of a near empty tank.

Although it may be good to know that you will not struggle to breathe until your last breath, one should thus note to more often check your SPG and not rely on a regulator to give resistance in breathing as a warning for a low tank pressure. This skill is often taught in open water classes to simulate the feeling of breathing from a tank with low gas supply and one may question the validity of the skill given modern dive gear, yes it has its place but should not be relied upon.

-Octopus regulator

Many divers will focus on a good primary regulator while forgetting about the octo or secondary regulator. From tests it was shown that single demand valve systems that meet breathing performance requirements (BS EN 250) may not be able to meet the same requirements when used as part of an 'Octopus' system.

This is sometimes due to low performance first stage regulators that cannot supply gas to two divers breathing in phase (at the same time). This can in cases explain why divers sometimes for no reason break contact with their buddies during an alternative air supply (AAS) ascent. Thus, divers need to realize that even though a first stage regulator is rated as EN250, it was tested for single use and it may not meet the demands of two divers breathing at the same time. Divers are to note the actual gas the regulator can deliver and should consider high flow regulator systems.

A study done by QinetiQ Ltd for the Health and Safety Executive (2005) on regulator systems divers normally purchased placed the systems in fresh water at a regulated temperature of 41 °F (5 °C) with breathing tests done at 0, 33, 66, 100, 132 and 165 ft (0, 10, 20, 30, 40 and 50 m) with a supplied pressure of 725 and 2175 psi (50 and 150 bar) to test for compliance with BS EN 12021:1999 standards. The study found that the first stage performance is a vital factor in the overall system performance and that even high flow secondary regulators could not meet the standards if used with a poor performing first stage, in addition that poor second stages could meet requirements when used with a high performance first stage regulator.

It was also noted that if the second stages were of different performance the two affected each other in performance. This can result in a diver being content with the breathing performance while being unaware that the buddy is having difficulty breathing. It is thus suggested that the same performance regulators are used in a system.

-Breathing together

It was noted that some systems would pass requirements when the divers breathed out of phase, but the moment both divers breathed at the same time the system had difficulty meeting the demand placed on it. Divers may perceive that the system has failed or that they have run out of air, and could result in panic. The change in performance is sudden (immediately upon breathing together) and would not give any warnings. It is noted that people close together (such as in gas sharing) have a tendency to synchronize their breathing.

Divers are thus urged to realize this and try not to breathe in phase in an emergency when poor performing systems are used. It should also be noted that older regulators, even if high flow and maintained correctly, lose performance and may not meet requirements over time.

-Tests on equipment after incidents

From a total of 54 incidents that involved 46 fatalities investigated by the Health and Safety Laboratory, it was found that almost half the regulators tested did not meet the performance requirements (EN 250). This was found to be due to lack of maintenance, servicing and cleaning, incorrect setup, and possible effects of mix and match of component parts.

-Going past 165 ft (50 m)

It should be noted that EN250 standards only test to 165 ft deep and that regulators may pass the test, however only marginally. The performance of a regulator may markedly fall below 165 ft deep.

-Too small a BCD

The size or lift capacity of the BCD is very important for deep diving, especially in cold places. If you are wearing a very thick wetsuit, you may need a lot of weight to be able to descend. As you descend, the wetsuit compresses and the buoyancy characteristics of the wetsuit change. Now you start to become heavy and the BCD needs to be able to cope with the added lift needed.

If you are wearing a drysuit, especially a crushed neoprene drysuit, then you are going to need a lot of weight to descend, if the drysuit seal breaks and the suit floods, your BCD now needs to be able to cope with the lift requirements to get you to the surface, taking too small a BCD may see you sink to the bottom. It has been reported from body recoveries (especially drysuit divers) that many of them still had their weights on when they were found. It seems in the panic divers do not always release their weights in an emergency (either due to an inability to think due to panic or Nitrogen narcosis).

Hoses

Few people notice that many hoses have a pressure rating themselves. This rating will be stamped into the hose and is normally the minimum burst pressure. Good quality original manufacture hoses normally have a high burst pressure, but there are hoses that have a low burst pressure as they were meant for shallow diving.

Another interesting discovery is that the plastics in some hose can be a source of contaminants. The US Navy reported (Naval Medical Research and Development Command report number NMRI- 92- 33) that it found toluene of 136 ppm surface equivalent contamination from air supply hoses making them unfit to use. Toluene is a solvent that is sometimes used as an inhalant drug due to its intoxicating properties, however when inhaling toluene it has the potential to cause severe neurological harm. It should also be noted that the solvents used to clean tanks and not properly washed out can contaminate a diver's gas supply and have possible damaging effects to the diver.

Scrubber poisoning

Many deep divers use CCR units, and of those soda lime is often used as a scrubber to remove CO2. It is interesting to note that in a study done, soda lime was found to be the source of ammonia (up to 30 ppm), ethyl and diethyl (up to several ppm) and various aliphatic hydrocarbons (up to 60 ppm). The researchers were unable to establish the exact reason for the contaminants but suggested that it may be due to the breakdown of the indicator dye ethyl violet used in some of the soda lime to indicate the decline of the soda lime. Due to this the US Navy has taken steps to use non dye indicating soda lime for their operations. (1996 Chemical safety of US Navy fleet soda lime, Undersea and Hyperbaric Medicine Vol 23 Number 1).

Dive computers

Doing dives below 130 ft normally involves going into decompression, many times using a higher content Oxygen mix for accelerated decompression and Tri-Mix mixtures for bottom gasses. You need specialized computers that can handle multiple gasses and Tri-Mix mixtures. The ability to change gasses underwater or amend your gas list is a handy function as you may need to breathe a gas other than your own in an emergency; often this gas is not in your gas list or part of your planning.

Dive computer depth limits are also a consideration; dive computers designed for recreational diving may not be able to handle the pressure for the depth you intend to dive to. In addition their decompression algorithms may not be as reliable or even be able to compute decompression for your depth. Depth accuracy is also a concern as most become more inaccurate at deeper depths. Readers are referred to 'Dive Computers' by Anton Swanepoel for more information on dive computer selection.

http://www.antonswanepoelbooks.com/dive_computers.php

Masks

Masks are often not a consideration for many divers; however they should be for deep divers. Low volume masks are often used by deep divers for the ease of equalizing the mask. However, low volume masks, especially ones with colored skirts, can make it difficult to see equipment close to the diver's body, normally in the chest and hip area. Many divers thus rather elect to use a higher volume mask, often with clear skirts or with lenses at the bottom to enable the diver to see gear easier.

Dive gauges

Dive gauges have a depth rating just like a flashlight. For deep diving you need to look for gauges that can handle the pressure. These will normally be oil-filled mechanical gauges. Expensive air-filled gauges should be able to handle 300 to 400 ft (90 to 120 m) however do not take chances and check the manufacturers' specifications. Another point to consider is Oxygen compatible pressure gauges for use in your decompression tanks containing an Oxygen content higher than 40%. Many people are so involved with Oxygen compatible regulators that they forget all about their pressure gauges.

Wetsuits

Due to the added pressure, wetsuits may not provide adequate insulation on deep dives. As you descend deeper, a 5mm wetsuit may end up being a 2mm wetsuit. Furthermore, note that some wetsuits may permanently compress if taken deep and lose most of its insulation properties. Even the best wetsuit will lose its thickness quicker on deep dives than if you only did shallow dives. A drysuit may be a better option for long-term use.

Travel mixes

With deeper dives on OC comes the problem of hypoxic back gas mixes. These mixes do not contain enough Oxygen to be safely used on the surface, in addition to if the dive were to be done on back gas from the surface; the gas used on the descent is taken from the gas supply intended for the bottom part of the dive. A small penalty in decompression is also incurred by using low Oxygen mixes for descent.

A solution is to have one or more mixes with a higher Oxygen content that is used for the descent part of the dive. These can be the same gas as that will be used on the ascent part of the dive or a different mix. However, if using a different mix, it does add to the risk of the diver breathing the wrong gas on either descent or ascent, in addition to the diver setting the dive computers to the wrong gas, computers need to be changed on the descent as the diver changes mixes to correctly reflect decompression time.

Having different mixes for ascent and descent also adds more cylinders to carry that can cause additional drag, especially in a current, but it does give the diver additional gas to breathe should a problem arise.

Some divers elect not to use travel tanks on the descending part of the dive, but to rather breath-hold down to a depth where the back gas can safely be breathed (normally around 20 ft). This reduces the risk of the diver setting the dive computers to the wrong gas or switching to the wrong gas, although as mentioned it does reduce the available bottom gas.

Chapter 13

Breathing for deep diving

Breathing is such a natural event that few people give it much consideration. Due to our modern world and our general lower level of inactivity, many people breathe incorrectly. At rest and for the daily tasks we often do (sitting behind a desk), this may be sufficient, although not optimal. However, underwater breathing correctly makes a huge difference in our ability to cope with the increased demand for Oxygen, not to mention extending our bottom time by conserving gas.

Breathing is largely an unconscious act, regulated by the body and linked to your fitness level and the level of exercise you are currently doing. The sole act of breathing is to deliver Oxygen to the body and eliminate CO_2 from the body. You can however consciously regulate your breathing, and in time even train your body to breathe differently.

Tidal volume

For a normal breath, you do not inhale and exhale the full capacity of your lungs, your lungs still have a reserve capacity and a residual volume. The amount of gas that you do inhale and exhale normally is called your tidal volume (TV). Although lung capacity does differ between people and also changes due to the type of exercise you do, TV averages around 6 to 8 milliliters (ml) per kilogram (kg) of body weight.

For a 70 kg person TV would be around 500 ml for each breath. Normal breathing is around 12 to 16 times a minute and around 4 to 8 times for very fit people. Thus a normal person with a TV of 500 ml would use around 6 to 7 liters (L) per minute at rest.

Reserve volume

The difference between the volume of air you take in while resting and the maximum volume of air you can take in when inhaling fully is called your reserve volume.

Residual volume

Even if you exhale all the air you can from your lungs, there will still be some air left in your lungs, preventing the lungs from falling flat when you exhale. This small amount of air still left in the lungs is called the residual volume.

Resting metabolism

At rest our body's metabolism is minimal, said to be around 70 to 100 calories an hour. Jup, that 100 calorie snack can keep you sitting at your desk for an hour. From studies it was noted that Oxygen consumption and TV at rest do not differ much between aerobically fit individuals and unconditioned individuals with the same body mass. Both TV and Oxygen consumption at rest is primarily determined by body mass.

Exercise and ventilation

Due to input from joints, muscles and other sensors, ventilation increases at the onset of exercise before arterial CO2 increases. The body is normally able to keep a constant arterial pressure of both O2 and CO2 during light and moderate exercise, however in extreme exercise arterial O2 partial pressure may decrease. For aerobically fit individuals only tidal volume increases with light to moderate exercise to cope with additional O2 demand and not the respiratory rate. The reason is that taking larger breaths is more efficient than taking faster shallower breaths, even though the same volume of air may be moved in a minute. With heavy and extreme exercise both tidal volume and breathing rate is increased.

Dead air space

Gas that remains in the airways (mouth, throat, windpipe and part of the lung) will not undergo gas exchange, this air is wasted and the areas that do not undergo gas exchange are called 'dead air space'. A regulator, snorkel and other breathing equipment add to the dead airspace.

Wasted air is around 2.2 ml/kg for the average person. For a 70 kg person that is around 150 ml of wasted air or 30% per breath. If 7 L is breathed every minute, then around 2.1 L of gas is lost. Since dead air space is fixed, it does not change with either increasing breathing rate or tidal volume. However, when the tidal volume is increased, a smaller percentage of gas is lost per breath. Even if the same 7 L was breathed per minute but in fewer breaths due to taking larger breaths, the percentage of wasted air would go down. For instance, if the resting tidal volume is increased form ½ L to 1 L per breath, only 150 ml will still be lost per breath; this drops the wasted percentage from 30 down to 15%. Thus, if the breaths were kept the same per minute (14 in this case) and the tidal volume doubled (from ½ L to 1 L) per breath, 2.1 L will still be lost in total per minute, however 14 L of air would have been moved. If the tidal volume however was kept at ½ L per breath and the number of breaths doubled, 4.2 L (30%) of air would have been wasted while moving the same 14 L of air.

One can then see why one is told to breathe deeper and slower in diving, as taking fewer but larger breaths is more efficient than taking smaller breaths. The work of breathing for larger breaths is also only slightly higher than smaller breaths due to the respiratory muscles only requiring a small increase in O2 consumption for larger breaths, up to the point where the metabolic cost of taking a larger breath will not be offset by increased Oxygen delivery to the system. The balance would be then to increase both tidal volume and respiratory rate in combination. Elite athletes have a tidal volume of around 60% of their vital capacity during maximal exercise.

Respiratory efficiency

With increased fitness, the body adapts and can extract more O2 from the same volume of air breathed. Thus fit people need less gas to support the equivalent level of exercise compared to unconditioned people.

At rest a person normally needs around 3.5 ml/kg/minute of O2, this will be around 250 ml/minute of O2 for a 70 kg individual. With air breathing, at rest and during submaximal exercise a person would need to breathe around 20 to 25 L of air for every liter of O2 consumed, called "the ventilatory equivalent". With aerobic conditioning ventilatory equivalent is reduced and less gas is needed to support a given level of exercise.

Breath-hold diving

Divers who participate in breath-hold diving have been known to have larger lungs after one year of repetitive breath-hold diving. This may seem as a bonus in decompression as larger lungs will have a larger surface area for gas exchange. However, more gas will not only diffuse out of the body at decompression, but more gas will also diffuse into the body at depth. Breath-hold divers also have the added problem of becoming resistant to higher levels of CO_2 and may have a higher resting level of CO_2 due to training the body to ignore warning messages for high levels of CO_2.

This can create the problem that a diver may exercise (swimming against a current) and build up a high level of CO_2 without feeling the effects of the added CO_2, then make a fast descent and pass out from CO_2 poisoning as the level of CO_2 was allowed to increase to a large amount before increased breathing would be triggered to lower the CO_2 level.

Increasing lung volume and effectiveness

The following exercises if practiced daily can help you increase your lung capacity and efficiency.

-Breathe deeply

To reduce the dead airspace percentage of inhaled air and increase the efficiency of the available gas you have underwater you need to increase your breath size by breathing deeper. Practice breathing deeper and exhale completely on every breath. To check if you are exhaling completely count out loud, if you cannot count any more, there is no more air to expel in your lungs.

Let your diaphragm descend by keeping your abdominal muscles relaxed, this will allow your abdomen to expand when your diaphragm descends, allowing more space for your lungs that in turn allows more air to fill them. Remember, two-thirds of your lungs are in the bottom half of your chest. You can also try to hold your arms away from your body to the sides (like a cross) and then pull your arms a bit back when you breathe in, helping to open up your chest. On exhale bring your arms forward again. Do this a few times each day to help you in learning to breathe deeper.

Do not try to breathe fast though, keep a constant slow pace. Note, in normal surface breathing a pace of two seconds inhale is normally advocated, however this pace is too fast for the volume of air that needs to be moved on deeper depths due to the gas density increasing. A five second inhalation with a one to two second pause followed by a five second exhalation is normally used underwater. For breathing at rest underwater some divers do an eight second inhale and exhale time, but this should not be done while exercising underwater as it could result in CO_2 build up. For on the surface breathing you can try to breathe in for 2-20 seconds and out for 10-20 seconds.

-Create resistance

Due to breathing underwater being done with increased resistance (denser breathing gas and breathing equipment), you can make your lungs more used to breathing with resistance. This not only helps make your lungs used to having to hold air longer, but also stretches them out, allowing more air to be taken in.

Try breathing out through your mouth while creating resistance with your lips by holding them together and only allowing air to escape under resistance. You can also blow up balloons with your lungs. These exercises are very useful for CCR divers who find it difficult to breathe on a CCR unit underwater. On a CCR unit the diver is the pump that pumps the gas around the loop, whereas in OC the regulator supplies gas under pressure to the diver. Thus, CCR divers usually have a slight negative breathing pressure, while OC divers normally have a slight positive breathing pressure.

Anton Swanepoel

-Exercise in water

Water is around 800 times denser than air and any movement done in water requires more energy and thus more Oxygen to make that energy. That Oxygen is supplied by the gas breathed in by the lungs. Try swimming or other water sports in making your body more used to water resistance, or make up an exercise route with some stretches and weight lifting in the routine, then practice it in the water. Stand at around neck level deep in water while lifting weights to your chest in front and from your hips up and out, like making a cross.

Due to the immersion effect, blood will shift to your chest cavity, increasing the compression on your body in addition to the water pressure and you will find that you cannot take as large breaths as normal. From research it was found that your air capacity can be cut by up to 75% during this time. The body will compensate for this reduction over time, resulting in your respiratory system being more efficient and your lung capacity increasing.

If you have no access to a swimming pool, you can compensate for it by training in a bathtub that is deep enough, although not as effectively. Fill the bath with water and lie down in it with the water covering your chest. Use small weights and hold them parallel to your body (on your sides), now bring them up using either an arm curl or by holding the arms straight. The basic idea is to do any exercise while in the water.

-Get additional air

Due to taking larger breaths causing some people to become lightheaded, you can practice this on land to help you cope underwater. This exercise will also help people that find it difficult breathing through their mouths.

Get a short (two to three inches) plastic pipe (clean) that will fit in your mouth. The pipe should be large enough to hold your mouth open reasonably wide without hurting you (about as wide as an average yawn). Note, do not use a long pipe as it will increase dead air space.

Breathe slowly and deeply for a few minutes every day. Note, if you breathe too quickly you may become lightheaded. In time you should be able to take very deep, full breaths without getting lightheaded as your body becomes used to the increased Oxygen it receives per breath.

-Play an instrument that uses your breath

Learn how to play a tuba, trumpet, trombone, oboe, clarinet, saxophone, harmonica or flute. This will help you with breath control in addition to expanding your lung capacity to utilize all the alveoli.

-Do rigorous cardiovascular activities

Cardiovascular sports such as aerobics, cycling, running, swimming and some dance routines improves your cardiovascular fitness in addition to raising your base metabolic rate. This increases your lung efficiency in addition to your decompression off-gassing. See 'Deep and Safety Stops, including Ascent Speed and Gradient Factors' for more information on this.
http://www.antonswanepoelbooks.com/deepstops.php

Note that swimming is the best all-round exercise. Swimmers can at peak exercise use Oxygen three times more efficiently than an average person.

-Stop smoking

Smoking not only damages your lungs, but irritates your mucus membranes including a host of other side effects; it just is not worth it. Try to also stay away from smoke-filled environments. This may require you to ask your partner to stop smoking and not to hang out with the smokers at work when they are smoking. The question is, how serious are you about your deep diving?

-Go snorkeling

With snorkeling you are not only enjoying the underwater scenery, but you are also learning to breathe through a snorkel that requires you to use your mouth for breathing. The snorkel also has some resistance in addition to dead air space, this requires you to breathe slower and deeper while building breathing muscle strength and increasing your lung volume.

-Special notes

Stop your exercise if you become lightheaded or you get a headache. Do not go swimming or snorkeling alone and do not do exercises in a pool alone. If you practice in a bathtub, be careful not to hurt yourself with the small space available. Never push yourself to exhaustion while training in water as you would in a gym, remember your heart works harder while underwater.

Always consult with your doctor before doing any exercise.

And above all, remember to have fun. ☺

Chapter 14

Fitness for deep diving

Deep diving places an immense workload on the body, not just from the ambient pressure and inert gas loads, but also from the long immersion in water, colder temperatures normally incurred, and possible dehydration. There is normally also additional gear that is heavier and more cumbersome to handle.

Thus deep diving divers normally need an increased level of fitness to cope with the stresses on the body for deep diving. However, interestingly there is a marked difference between people that do aerobic exercises (such as long-distance running and swimming) than people that do anaerobic exercises (such as weight lifting).

In a study done by NASA to determine the effects of exercise on DCS risk before altitude exposure, an interesting link was noted between exercise type and DCS risk. It was noted that subjects that regularly perform anaerobic exercises had a higher DCS incidence than subjects that do aerobic exercises.

Aerobic exercise such as long-distance running, cycling or swimming is seen to raise the basal metabolic rate and may increase Nitrogen elimination on decompression and reduce DCS risk. It should not be seen that doing anaerobic exercise places one at increased risk, but that having a higher basal metabolic rate reduces DCS risk. In one case a student made regular runs or swimming exercises daily. When he started studying for exams he was inactive and four months later started incurring skin itching and post dive fatigue after dives that he had no problem with before.

Note that exercising after decompression is seen to increase DCS risk.

Smoking and deep diving

Many divers know that smoking is not good for them, but pay only lip service to the warnings. This is largely due to the addiction to smoking being stronger than the fear of what smoking does to you.

The following are a few side effects of smoking that have relevance to diving, although smoking has other health damaging effects.

-Irritants

The irritants in tobacco cause immediate coughing and broncoconstriction that inhibit cilliary action (microscopic hairs that remove harmful particles) in the lungs while stimulating mucus secretion. This reduces gas transfer in the lungs and may cause a mucus blockage. The exposure to nicotine causes an increase in nicotinic cholinergic receptors in the brain, resulting in structural and functional changes in the brain and nervous system.

On long dives (and sometimes even one hour dives) withdrawal symptoms occur that induce physical and psychological changes in the person that can lead to mistakes in decision making or cutting deco and safety just to get out of the water sooner in order to have a smoke. People have been known to fill their BCD with cigarette smoke before a dive to allow them to breathe the gas in and out while underwater, so desperate are they for nicotine.

Irritants in tobacco smoke induce a chronic inflammation of the alveoli that results in the production of proteolytic enzymes that eat away at the alveolar wall, reducing its strength including ventilation-perfusion abnormalities (reduced gas exchange). The forced expiratory volume in one second (FEV1), or the amount of gas you can expel in one second, is reduced to 80% in most average smokers. Forced vital capacity (FVC), or the amount you can exhale from a full inhale to a full exhale, is reduced by 10% on average and is seen as a significant indication of lung dysfunction. This will result in a reduction in pulmonary gas exchange in decompression (increased DCS risk) and may predispose a diver to lung over expansion injuries even at very low pressures.

-Nicotine

Nicotine also promotes platelet aggregation and fibrinogen formation that are precursors to blood clotting and can obstruct small blood vessels increasing total peripheral resistance, heart rate and blood pressure. From studies it was shown that circulation in small blood vessels is reduced by 19% after only two cigarettes. A rise in peripheral resistance (closing or restriction of small blood vessels) of around 20 to 30% occurs in the presence of nicotine. Since gas exchange occurs in the small blood vessels, a reduction of circulatory efficiency in this area will have a significant effect on decompression.

Nicotine withdrawal due to not smoking as regularly, especially underwater, causes severe performance degradation, memory impairment, confusion, impulsiveness and slowed reaction time. In a stressful event, the diver may not be able to make simple decisions to save his/her life. Smoking also increases mucus production, increases pulse rate and blood pressure, lowers body temperature, causes a constriction on blood vessels and increase breathing rate.

-CO

Oxygen in the blood is largely carried by hemoglobin with a small amount dissolved in the blood. As the local tissues use Oxygen, the dissolved Oxygen in the blood replaces the used Oxygen in the tissues. Oxygen bound to the hemoglobin is then released to replace the dissolved Oxygen in the blood that was used up. This forms part of the 'Oxygen Window' effect. For more information on Oxygen window and decompression see my book: 'Deep and Safety Stops, including Ascent Speed and Gradient Factors'.

If the level of CO2 in the body rises, the body reacts by increasing ventilation (under normal circumstances) and initiates the release of more Oxygen to the tissues by reducing the hemoglobin affinity for Oxygen, allowing easier Oxygen release (shift to the right).

If the levels of CO in the body rise, the reverse will happen (shift to the left). CO binds around 250 times better to hemoglobin, creating a compound called carboxyhemoglobin and prevents Oxygen binding to hemoglobin. Carboxyhemoglobin levels in smokers are around 15% and in non-smokers around 1%. The affinity of hemoglobin for Oxygen is also increased, making it harder for hemoglobin that is carrying Oxygen to release it when reaching the tissues, resulting in possible hypoxia (reduced Oxygen). For smokers, up to 15% of the Oxygen in your blood can be replaced by CO.

-Effects of chronic hypoxia

Chronic hypoxia causes increased production of red blood cells in an effort to increase Oxygen transport. Normal red blood cells are around 35 to 40% of blood by volume and increases by around 20% in smokers. The increased volume of red blood cells causes an increase in blood viscosity (thicker) that affects the circulation, with sludging of blood in capillaries in addition to damaging the cells lining the blood vessels (endothelium). The damage to the cell lining creates a local inflammation response that causes swelling and further reduction in blood flow as the vessel size narrows. Any bubbles in the blood that may normally have passed, may now become stuck or scrape against the blood vessel wall, creating further cell damage, possibly leading to blood complement activation (around 20 proteins) that plays a major role in DCS. For more on blood complement activation see: 'Deep and Safety Stops, including Ascent Speed and Gradient Factors'.

-Hydrogen cyanide

Hydrogen cyanide is one of the chemicals found in tobacco smoke and directly prevents the use of Oxygen by cells due to interference with mitochondria found in cells, in addition to causing direct injury to the lungs. The gas interferes with the alveolar enzymes in the lungs that are normally responsible for maintaining the integrity of the alveolar membranes. Even small amounts of hydrogen cyanide are deadly.

-Hydrogen sulfide

Hydrogen sulfide also found in tobacco smoke is a direct toxin, especially for tissues it directly contacts such as the lungs, and causes immense damage to cells.

-Mucous production

Smoking causes nasal and sinus drainage problems in most divers which can increase the chance for middle ear and sinus blocks resulting in reverse blocks or squeezes. It takes about seven days after stopping smoking for mucous production to return to normal, thus stopping a day or so before a deep dive is not enough, and in some tests it has been noted that mucus production actually increases directly after stopping smoking.

Drugs and deep diving

Few drugs in use today have been tested for their effects under pressure or elevated pressures of Oxygen. Certain drugs are unpredictable as to their effects on the human body while diving, with side effects being either subtle or strong in addition to being variable. Divers should seek medical advice from diving doctors or Divers Alert Network when taking prescription drugs before diving.

However, few divers think twice when taking decongestants and motion sickness medication while diving. Some decongestants contain pseudoephedrine that can affect the heart and blood pressure and is contraindicated for diving. Other side effects include drowsiness, memory problems, inability to concentrate, and mood changes. Decongestant medications are normally antihistamine medication that provides relief by constricting blood vessels to reduce tissue swelling and can increase DCS risk in addition to often causing drowsiness and decreased mental acuity. Most motion sickness medications are also antihistamine medication that can cause the same symptoms as mentioned above, in addition to functional motor impairment, sedative effects and blurred vision.

Although these symptoms can cause problems in recreational diving, on a deep dive where the option to terminate the dive and surface immediately is not an option, it can create a great risk. Test medication before making a dive, especially a deep dive, to see the effects it has on you.

Fatty food and deep diving

Most people love fatty foods, since it is so gratifying and makes us feel fuller for longer. However, how does that fatty meal affect your body, especially that bacon and sausage in the morning and hamburger for lunch before a dive?

-One meal is all it takes

Dr. Travis Stork did a study to see what the effects are on a healthy person after eating only one fatty meal. Dr. Stork used two healthy 19 year old females for his tests. Directly after eating the meals, Caroline the female that ate the healthy meal felt very good and full of energy, while Celina the female that ate the fatty meal was tired and just wanted to sleep.

From the blood tests it showed that the fatty meal was harder to digest, stressing the body. Celina's triglycerides (the chemical form in which most fat exists in food as well as in the body) doubled after the meal and her heart was working 30% harder while her arteries were less compliant (flexible). If we couple this with the fact that immersion in water increases the work load of the heart by itself and raises blood pressure, the fatty meal is not looking so good. A shocking result was that Celina's blood was actually literally curdled (blood cells clumping, slowing down circulation and can stop blood flow in small blood vessels). Her blood was also cloudy from fat in the blood. These fatty deposits can cause bubble formation by creating nuclei seeds including possibly blocking small blood vessels.

-Effects of fatty food on memory and energy

Fatty food also affects memory and exercise performance, however over the long term it has a destructive effect on the body. From tests done on 32 rats that were first fed a low-fat diet containing 7.5% fat and then later a diet containing 55% fat, it was found that memory performance sharply degraded after only four days.

Rats had to negotiate a maze and find 8 treats (condensed milk), the rats found all or seven of the treats without making a mistake by doubling back on itself. However, when the rats' diet was changed to a higher fat one, they only found on average five treats before making a mistake after four days on the high fat diet.

The same rats were also tested with treadmill exercises, and it was found after five days that performance on fatty meals dropped by half. One theory for the sharp decline in performance and memory is that fat can trigger insulin resistance making the body less efficient at using glucose that is the only energy the brain can use. The thought is that the body reacts to a high fat content in the blood by releasing proteins that essentially slows down and reduces metabolism efficiency. This is thought to be a protective mechanism of the body in order to get rid of excess fat and not store it; however, the effect is that muscles are less efficient at using Oxygen and fuel to make energy.

From new research published in July 4, 2011 it was noted that fatty foods cause the body to produce a natural feel-good chemical, similar to the effect of marijuana. This effectively encourages overeating and addiction.

-Conclusion

Thus after only one fatty meal your heart is stressed and has to work harder, your blood is thicker and sludge's for up to 8 hours, while your arteries become stiffer, your memory and performance is compromised. Combine that with a cup of coffee and sugar with being unfit and we see why heart attack is such a big problem in diving.

Caffeine and deep diving

Caffeine is such a part of our daily life that few people stop to wonder at the effects it has on us.

-Effects of caffeine on the body

Caffeine is a stimulant drug that acts on the central nervous system by temporarily warding off drowsiness and restoring alertness. Although caffeine is toxic at higher doses, normal consumption of a few cups of coffee a day has little known health risks, even if consumed for years. Some people do however have trouble sleeping after consuming caffeine, while others are not affected and most build up a tolerance to caffeine with regular use. For new users, caffeine normally causes a diuretic effect (need to urinate).

-Lethal dose

Consumption of over 250 mg caffeine per day can lead to caffeinism which can cause nervousness, irritability, restlessness, insomnia, headaches, and heart palpitations. Intake of over 300 mg caffeine can cause anxiety. With an extreme intake, caffeine overdose can result in death; however the amount needed is around 150 to 200 milligrams caffeine per kilogram body mass, or about 80 to 100 cups of normal instant coffee for an average adult (instant coffee contains around 80 to 100 milligram per cup).

Although this would require some hard drinking, deaths have been reported from caffeine pills with overdosing that required hospitalization with as little as 2 grams of caffeine (the average caffeine pill contains 200mg). The caffeine pills seem to be more effectively taken up into the blood stream than drinking coffee. Caffeine pills are used for weight loss, pick-me-ups, and body building.

Certain drugs such as fluvoxamine (an antidepressant) and levofloxacin can increase the effects of caffeine five fold by blocking liver enzymes that metabolize caffeine, creating a lower tolerance for caffeine overdose. Fluvoxamine also reduces the clearance of caffeine by more than 90%, and prolongs its elimination half-life (the time it takes to clear half the amount of caffeine from the system) more than tenfold; from 4.9 hours to 56 hours.

Caffeine overdose death is normally due to ventricular fibrillation due to caffeine's effects on the cardiovascular system.

-How caffeine keeps you awake
In the brain, caffeine reduces the effects of adenosine due to the caffeine molecule being structurally similar to adenosine, allowing it to bind to adenosine receptors on the surface of cells without activating them.

Although adenosine is found throughout the body due to neuron activity, its function in the brain is to protect the brain by suppressing neural activity and increasing blood flow. Adenosine is thought to be involved in the control of the sleep-wake cycle, and accumulation of adenosine in the brain may be a primary cause of sleepiness due to prolonged mental activity. As the levels of adenosine rise in the body, your body will start to nudge you to bed. Since caffeine bonds with the adenosine receptors without activating it, the body does not pick up that adenosine levels are high and keeps you going. Caffeine may also increase fat utilization and decrease muscle glycogen utilization, enhancing endurance performance.

Although caffeine does not directly increase brain power, it keeps the body awake and going which may be temporarily useful for tasks that are learned and require little thinking, however tasks that require reasoning and thought may be degraded.

Note that from tests it was found that certain drinks had no increased endurance against a placebo and may be a result of how the coffee beans are made, in the same tests however caffeine pills had a 10 times increase in performance. This does not offset the long term change to the body of caffeine use, and increased energy could also be had from healthy eating.

When you are tired and need to do relatively straightforward work that does not require lots of thinking, coffee has been shown to help increase output and quality in addition to improve declarative memory creation and retention (remembering lists or answers to exam questions).

-Caffeine addiction

Caffeine causes blood sugar (glucose) to be released that creates the quick fix caffeine users love, however this requires your pancreas to over-work to produce extra insulin to reduce the extra blood sugar released. When all the blood sugar is used up, the quick fix is over and your body starts to crave for the next fix, normally resulting in you feeling more tired than before the caffeine quick fix as the body used up reserve energy to keep you going and produce more insulin. Note that caffeine normally reaches the blood stream 30 to 45 minutes after consumption.

Over time, the pancreas constantly creates additional insulin in anticipation of the added sugar, resulting in blood sugar you need to feel alert and energetic being removed before you can use it. This will make you feel tired and in need of more blood sugar, the result more caffeine as a quick get me out of bed and a vicious cycle is born. The blocking of adenosine receptors will prevent deep sleep even if you think you have a restful night's sleep, resulting in you waking feeling tired, thus you reach for a wake me up cup of coffee. This will start a cycle that is hard to break. Apples are a more natural wake me up way.

In a study done in 1995 it was shown that people become tolerant to daily caffeine intake after around a week to 12 days. In one test some participants getting 900 milligrams per day found that the caffeine users had nearly identical mood, energy, and alertness levels after 18 days of use compared to placebo participants.

-Caffeine and your heart

Studies show that heart rate is increased with around 15 to 20 beats per minute after consuming two cups of caffeine. Stress hormones rose by 32% with 4 cups of coffee. Due to diving already placing added stress on the heart, increased heart rate and blood pressure from caffeine can (especially for unfit individuals) increase the risk of heart failure.

-Caffeine and decompression

Although caffeine may increase heart rate and possibly blood flow that may have an effect on gas uptake and release, the withdrawal symptoms are more of a problem. When headaches occur due to caffeine withdrawal, the blood vessels in the brain are constricted due to caffeine and may hinder off-gassing that can increase CNS DCS in the brain.

Studies have also shown that caffeine can modify regional blood flow due to altering the cardiovascular response to dynamic exercise and thus can affect gas diffusion and decompression.

Fat tissue blood flow is directly linked to blood pressure, thus when the blood pressure increases, blood flow and gas diffusion to fatty tissue is increased. As the caffeine works out, blood pressure and heart rate will return to normal, lowering blood pressure and reducing perfusion to fatty tissue.

The result is that on-gassing is increased in the bottom part of a dive to fatty tissue and possibly reduced at the decompression part of the dive if the dive is long enough (although caffeine half life is normally in the range of four hours, some people metabolize it very fast, also the tolerance effect will cause your body to react less to a lower level of caffeine in the body).

-Withdrawal symptoms
For diving, withdrawal symptoms are mostly the biggest problem of caffeine users. For deep divers, divers may go some time without having a cup of coffee or other caffeine containing drinks that can lead to withdrawal symptoms which include headache, irritability, inability to concentrate, drowsiness, insomnia, and pain in the stomach, upper body, and joints. (Note, many sports drinks contain caffeine).

This may adversely affect the diver underwater and can lead the diver to make mistakes due to not being able to concentrate or being irritated. Although withdrawal symptoms normally appear within a few hours of discontinuing caffeine intake, it normally peaks at around 48 hours and can last up to five days.

Sugar and deep diving
So now that we have seen how caffeine can affect you during diving, let's see how those sweet white and brown crystals in your coffee and tea compound the effects. Before you sink into despair about having to stop consumption of sugar, take note that your body does require sugar (glucose) to function as it is the only fuel your brain can use, however the body is able to produce all the glucose the brain needs through the digestion of whole, natural, unprocessed foods. Thus a little sugar may give a small boost, but too much is not good.

-Speed is the problem
Fruits, milk and whole grains contain natural sugars that the body breaks down slowly into glucose. Due to the slow release, the glucose is burned smoothly and gradually creating a sustained energy and not sudden spikes.

As insulin production is not rapidly increased to handle a large sudden increase in blood sugar levels, the body is in a natural state.

Refined sugar is to the body what nitrous is to a car. It enters the blood stream at a very fast rate and is burned very fast, creating an upsurge of energy until the sugar is used up, then just as in a car when the nitrous runs out, everything slows down. Since refined sugar itself has no minerals or vitamins that are required for its processing, it strips the body of these vital components and stresses the body while accelerating the degenerative processes.

The hypothalamus in the brain registers glucose levels and when an excess amount is detected it prepares for the increase in glucose by increasing insulin production in the pancreas. However, the glucose does not arrive at the hypothalamus as whatever glucose was going to arrive has already been utilized by the body or bound in tissues unavailable to the body due to the fast burn rate of sugar. This has the same result as caffeine with increased insulin production; however the two together create a larger spike and also a larger drop with a big crash and burn at the end. Sugar, as with caffeine, can also create addiction and depression (due to insulin depressing the system and the lack of endorphins in the brain).

Note, of all the foods consumed today, refined sugar is thought to be one of the most harmful.

Immersion Pulmonary Edema (IPE)

Immersion Pulmonary Edema (IPE) is a rare but potentially life-threatening condition where a diver or surface swimmer's lungs accumulate fluid. In scuba diving it was first reported in a group of divers by Wilmshurst in 1984. Although IPE is more common in cold water, it does occur in warmer waters. The number of cases is on the increase and IPE poses a serious risk for scuba divers, apnea divers, and long distance swimmers. In a survey with USA Triathlon Organization (USAT) members, 1,400 responses were received and a 1.4% prevalence of IPE was calculated. In military combat swimmers a prevalence of 1.8% was reported.

A survey of 1,250 divers found a 1.1% response with symptoms that suggest pulmonary edema was the result. With millions of divers diving, many can be at risk and divers doing deep dives should take note of any strange feelings in the chest or difficulty in breathing before and during the dive.

-What happens

The exact cause of IPE is not known but currently the theory is that when the body is immersed in water a redistribution of blood occurs with blood from the legs and arms going to the central cavity (around 700 ml). The blood pressure in the right atrium increases by around 16-18 mmHg and cardiac output increases around 30%.

Normally the heart and lungs compensate for the increase, however in some cases the increased pressure within the blood vessels of the lungs is so great that stress failure of the pulmonary capillaries occurs due to the blood-gas barrier (formed by the capillary endothelium, alveolar epithelium, and the extracellular matrix (ECM)) being extremely thin in order to allow diffusion of Oxygen and carbon dioxide.

At first pore stretching of the capillary endothelial cell may occur that causes larger molecules (such as hemoglobin) to move into the interstitium of the alveolar wall. At higher pressures stress failure of the blood-gas barrier results and fluid crosses the barrier that contains a high protein content approaching that of blood (resembling drowning). This can occur within minutes of immersion. The effect can also occur due to an underwater myocardial infarction (heart attack) or from abnormalities of the heart muscle, heart valves or hypertension (high blood pressure).

Due to cold water causing vasoconstriction and increased flow resistance to blood, it may predispose a person to IPE. The effects of vasoconstriction can be increased in addition to further vasoconstriction due to high blood pressure, smoking, caffeine, exertion and other factors that increase blood pressure or vasoconstriction, including possibly high O2 breathing as it causes vasoconstriction and bronchi construction.

A study done by Miller found that not only was hypertension and long-distance swims a risk factor, but so too the use of fish-oil supplements and the use of a wetsuit in swimming (possibly due to the restriction they apply to the limbs). Pulmonary over inflation due to breath-holding on ascent, malfunctioning regulators, or not correctly venting a rebreather loop allowing pressure to build up in the loop, is thought to increase the risk of IPE.

Negative pressure breathing is also seen to increase the risk of IPE due to it increasing the pressure ratio between the blood and lung pressure.

Negative pressure pulmonary edema can occur due to acute airway obstruction (tight wetsuit or physical airway obstruction), breathing against a high resistance regulator, scuba valve failure, low tank air pressure, tank valve not turned completely on, breathing a dense gas at depth, faulty regulators (scuba tanks filled in places containing volcanic dust in the air has resulted in regulator malfunctions), and rebreathers (cases from CCR divers have been reported and are thought to be due to the effort needed by the diver sucking the gas through the loop).

-Symptoms

Divers may feel short of breath (often after only a few minutes in the water), a sensation of not getting enough air while at depth, coughing, fatigue, dyspnea, weakness, expectoration of froth, chest discomfort, orthopnea, wheezing, hemoptysis (coughing up bloodstained sputum from the bronchi), dizziness, unconsciousness and death. A significant reduction in arterial O2 may be present, although IPE is not associated with decompression diving.

Symptoms sometimes occur while still on the surface, especially if a diver had to do a surface swim against a current. On ascent divers will experience no improvement and can cough up pink, frothy sputum. The fluid can reduce the amount of Oxygen reaching the blood which in turn can result in other symptoms such as panic or unconsciousness. Breathing may be noisy. Although the symptoms can seem like cardiac arrest, chest pain is usually absent in IPE.

Symptoms and signs normally resolve by themselves in 24 to 48 hours in mild cases, however severe cases may take longer even with hospitalization. However, in all cases divers should see a doctor for a checkup and not return to diving until after being cleared by a doctor. Deaths have been noted where divers experienced edema with difficulty breathing yet continued diving the next day where the diver collapsed after the first dive. Although medical treatment was given, the patient succumbed due to the fluid in the lungs.

-Treatment

The individual should be removed from the water as soon as possible and given Oxygen to breathe, preferably from a continuous flow mask not a demand regulator if possible. In advanced cases hospitalization and possibly CPR would be required. Diuretics may in some cases be used due to their immediate effect (such as intravenous furosemide). Recompression therapy is not given for IPE unless it occurs with another malady that requires hyperbaric Oxygen therapy.

-Edema and breath-hold diving

A study was done on 19 participants at an international breath-hold diving competition. Edema signs were found in 12 divers after deep dives ranging 82.5-247.5 ft (25–75 m) with none experiencing any symptoms or signs with shallow pool dives. Average reductions of around 9 to 12% were noted in both forced vital capacity (FVC) and forced expiratory volume in the first second (FEV1) in all 19 divers in addition to a 4% reduction noted in Oxygen saturation (SaO2) after deep dives.

This study is the first to show a reduced spirometric performance and arterial hypoxemia due to deep breath-hold diving thought to be due to diving induced pulmonary edema. Deep breath-hold diving is thus associated with an increased risk of pulmonary edema.

Chapter 15

Pre-dive readiness and relaxation

The pace you set before a dive and the state your mind is in affects your dive to a large extent, in addition your ability to respond to emergencies.

Running around like a headless chicken before a dive will only result in you forgetting important steps in the gear-up, in addition to possibly making mistakes in dive planning and maybe not enjoying the dive as it feels rushed and not relaxed. Feeling stressed is not the way you want to feel deep down. It is best to remain calm and handle problems step by step, focusing on what needs to be fixed now.

Many tech divers take a few minutes before a dive to calmly imagine the whole dive in their minds. They visualize how they will enter the water and descend, complete the bottom portion of the dive including any line laying or penetration that needs to be done. For the ascent they visualize switching to the correct gas at each depth and setting their computers correctly. They also visualize any problems that can occur (such as a burst hose or free flowing regulator) and how they calmly respond to those emergencies.

This creates a calmer and clearer mind that will allow you to see problems easier before it causes an emergency, in addition to allowing you to react calmer and possibly faster to an emergency.

Many divers also take up calming exercises such as yoga, Pilates or stretching exercises.

If you cannot obtain a clear and calm mindset before a dive, then it is advised to not do the dive. Many divers have been injured or died when someone in the group had a bad feeling. If something feels wrong about the dive, listen to your inner voice. This also goes for if you are struggling with accepting a bad experience. If a family member died, you lost your job, or you and your partner broke up recently, it is not a good idea to go diving, let alone deep diving. Divers may become sad underwater when they have time to think and suicidal thoughts can occur at depth, especially if the diver is under heavy narcosis. Remember, mental state has an effect on narcosis and can worsen the effects the diver feels.

Anton Swanepoel

Chapter 16

Survival mindset

Whether you think you can succeed or not, you are correct. Divers have given up in situations that seemed hopeless to them, used their last minutes of gas to write a goodbye note, while the exit was a short distance away.

Realize that with deep diving, gear, diving practices and knowledge are normally pushed to the limits, what can go wrong will one day go wrong.

Learning for deep diving

There are differences in learning for deep diving. You can learn to just get the rating and the plastic card and wall certificate, or you can learn to understand.

-Shallow learning

In shallow learning information is memorized so as to pass an exam, and skills are done in a robot like fashion where they are just a repeat motion of what was shown by the instructor. Only what needs to be done is done and the end goal of doing the course is not to learn why a skill is done or why information is given to learn, but the ticket that allows the diver to go deeper. The question often asked is, what do I have to do to go deeper, followed by is there not a shorter way. Trainees often try to set rules and procedures in place for expected situations without developing plans that are flexible so that they can adapt to changes.

-Deep learning

In deep learning the diver wants to learn more than what is normally offered, the diver is more engaging in the class and wants to know the theory and the reason behind skills so as to help the diver understand why a skill is done. This will also help the diver in emergency situations where a new procedure may need to be used other than what is learned to solve a problem. The diver becomes a thinking diver and realizes that the instructor cannot give skills and solutions for every possible problem the diver will face, and that skills that are learned are to be viewed like a toolbox full of tools. Each skill learned is like an individual tool that can be used in a variety of situations, not just those that were learned in the class. Divers also want to understand how the environment affects them. It is not just a goal to get a ticket to go deep, but a goal to go safely deep.

The diver becomes more flexible and understands that things do not always go as planned and plans for this. Thus the diver is normally calmer when things go wrong and also more capable of creating solutions as the diver realized beforehand that it could happen and mentally trained for it.

-Mistakes in classes

Many divers think that they are failures when taking a class if they cannot perform a skill the first time. Others pat themselves on the back for performing a skill the first time. Although it may be cool to be able to do a skill first time around, there are some drawbacks to this. Take for example a mask remove, replace and clear exercise. If the first diver does it perfectly the first time, the diver would have had one practice experience.

If the second diver tries and fails, maybe gets some water in the nose and panics but recovers or tries again, then the diver had multiple experiences. The second diver may do it a few times before reaching pass level, however that diver just moved past a mental block that the first dive may have but never realized. The second diver may in a real life situation not do it as perfectly, but if the diver again gets a little water in the nose, the diver may not panic as the diver has experienced it before. The mask clear could be messy in an emergency situation, but the diver may remain calm

The first diver that never experienced water in the nose may in an emergency or mishap underwater try to clear the mask and get water in the nose, possibly causing panic as this situation has not been encountered before.

Thus for survival, there is no such thing as too much practice if done right and there is much to be learned from divers that struggle with a skill. If you did the skills right, ask yourself how you would react if what happens with a struggling diver happens to you, in addition to asking yourself what if something does happen and you cannot do the skill perfectly, how will you react, for some divers are perfectionists that get mad if they struggle to do a skill. Thus will you remain calm or get frustrated and mad when you struggle underwater with a problem? Be prepared and survive.

Staying focused

Even with short dives things do not always work out, and in technical diving things rarely go exactly as planned, although mostly close to it. Staying focused on the moment and what needs to be done in that moment will help you through. Solve each problem as they come up. When things do not go as planned, it's up to you to find new solutions to your problems.

Anton Swanepoel

Staying alive

Although this is not a survival book, every technical diver should realize that they may find themselves in a situation where they may see no reason to keep going or to stay alive or no solution to their problem.

Know that every person will one day depart this earth and it is because we will die that life has meaning to us and every moment we are alive is precious. We do not know when death will come or how, nor can you take any possession with you. What matters in the end is not how rich you were, it is how you lived your life and the decisions you made and how you treated other people. Did you use your position of power to help others, or to oppress and hurt others? To stay alive you need a reason to stay alive that is more powerful than the obstacles you face. Many people have survived seemingly impossible circumstances, while others have perished in minor events.

Your reason to stay alive may be seeing loved ones again, to live life to its fullest, or to do right to those you wronged. Knowing that life is a precious gift and that how you spend every moment is what counts, will help you in finding a reason to stay alive.

While you are still alive, the possibilities remain unlimited.

Chapter 17

Never leave your wingman

Complacency and pride have killed more divers than should have died normally. Divers after some time start to take things for granted and make assumptions, assumptions that can get them or their buddy killed.

When divers dive together for some time, especially when they are experienced divers, the risk is there that divers think their buddy is OK and would ask for help if they wanted it. However, divers forget that their buddy may not be in a state where they are able to ask for help and may not even realize they are in trouble themselves. Some divers also assume that their buddy will make it to the surface and do not always ascend with their buddy, only to find that their buddy did not make it, and never will.

Following are three occurrences to make one think a bit.

Incidence one:

It was a calm day with beautiful clear Caribbean water making for an awesome dive. The dive was the first dive of a two tank boat dive with twelve guests and two diving instructors in the water. The captain of the boat who was also the instructor leading the group, had more than eight years experience as a dive guide. The second instructor who was at the rear of the group to assist with any divers in trouble had more than five years experience as a dive guide in addition to being a technical instructor (OC Tri-Mix), technical cave diver and wreck instructor.

On descent, one of the customers had a regulator failure as his alternate second stage started free flowing and could not be stopped. The guide taking up the rear was about to check his gear to enter the water when the customer returned to the boat. The instructor helped the customer to replace his tank with a full one in addition to replacing the malfunctioning regulator set with a spare set from the boat. By this time the other divers had already descended and the two divers quickly followed. The second instructor did notice that the gas in his tank had a slight smell to it but it was not strong nor did it taste bad, in addition to no one else commenting on foul gas, thus he entered the water without thinking any more about it. The group was at 100 ft when the two divers caught up with them.

After around ten minutes the guide started to slowly ascend to make a multi-level dive. At this point, the instructor in the rear started to feel unwell with a headache coming on. The leader turned the dive around at around 15 minutes due to a customer signaling that he had used half of his gas supply. The group was now at 60 ft on top of the wall and swimming back to the boat. At this stage, the instructor in the back was starting to feel really ill and tried to get the leader's attention by banging on his tank with a steel clip. The leader unfortunately was wearing a hooded vest and could not hear the other instructor. The second instructor's condition rapidly deteriorated to the point that he was not able to tell the difference on his computer between the depth and dive time even though he had used it on more than a thousand dives. The instructor realizing that something was very wrong, inflated his BCD and made a slow buoyant ascent, almost losing consciousness on the way up.

On the surface the instructor nearly passed out, and it took him ten minutes before he was in a state to swim back to the boat. The instructor leading the dive had by this time led the group to the boat and swam off on his own to have a look over the wall in case a shark or eagle ray was passing by. The leading instructor did not try to locate his colleague when he got to the boat as he assumed his colleague was very experienced and could take care of himself.

When the leading instructor returned to the boat, most of the guests had already ascended and as the instructor did not see his colleague with the remaining divers, he assumed his colleague must have ascended earlier. Only on returning to the boat did the first instructor learn that his colleague had been in trouble and nearly drowned. On testing the tank gas it was found that the gas was contaminated as the compressor filters malfunctioned and oil was allowed to pass through. The tanks affected were all enriched air tanks, and the leading instructor used a tank that was filled before the failure, and all the guests used air on the boat on that day. On inspection of the tanks left at the resort and the additional enriched air tanks on the boat a number were found to be contaminated. Although the gas smelled and tasted only marginally different than the other tanks, which may explain why the dive guide dove with it, the gas had a marked effect on the diver.

Incidence two:
Two friends, John and Pat, made a dive on a wreck that sat in the sand at 130 ft with most of the interesting parts of the wreck at 100 to 110 ft. Although they have been diving together for five years, logging over 300 dives, only John had dived the wreck before. John wanted to show his friend the whole wreck and kept a quick pace. Although he did note that Pat was struggling to keep up, he ignored it as his friend did not signal that he needed help.

After 20 minutes on the wreck, they were back at the anchor line and signaled to each other that it was time to ascend. John led the ascent, but did not pay much attention to Pat. John last saw Pat at around 40 ft and although he made his safety stop without Pat, he never thought anything was amiss. It was only on surfacing that John realized Pat was not with him or on the boat, and alerted the captain. A divemaster immediately entered the water, however due to the depth, he was unable to do an extensive search. Help was summoned from technical divers with the gear, training and gas to make the deep search. However, it took an hour for the divers to reach the dive site due to the distance needed to travel. Pat's body was recovered six hours later.

Pat's scuba cylinder was empty, he had a broken fin strap, and his weights were still in place. The medical investigation found death by drowning. It is thought that Pat's fin strap may have broken on the dive and could be the reason why he was having trouble keeping up. It is also possible that he built up an excess amount of CO_2 and suffered from the effects that would have made his narcosis far worse, and he may not have been in a state to signal that he was having trouble. However, he was able to ascend and make it to 40 ft where he was last seen. When he ran out of air is unknown, and although it is noted that he should have alerted his buddy that he was low on air, his buddy may have noted he was in trouble had he ascended with him. Even if Pat was still affected by narcosis and CO_2 poisoning and could not think to inform his buddy that he was out of gas, his buddy would have seen him pass out if they ascended together and may have been able to bring him to the surface where he may have been rescued.

Incidence three:
Two dive instructors who worked with each other and often dived together were doing a night dive at one of their favorite sites. John was leading with Cindy following. Cindy was an instructor for only a year with two years diving experience. John had been an instructor for four years and was also a technical instructor. From John's experience to monitor his student's gas supply at depth he had a habit of even checking his buddy's air consumption, for as he puts it, "At 330 ft even a minute of rapid breathing wastes a lot of gas." John noted that Cindy was breathing quickly even though the pace was very slow and told her to calm down and breathe deeper and slower.

After around 10 minutes of dive time when Cindy was still breathing fast and shallow, John decided that something must be wrong and signaled to Cindy that they must ascend. Cindy was reluctant at first but John insisted. They were at 60 ft at this point and made a slow ascent with John watching Cindy closely.

When they surfaced, Cindy was barely able to breathe so out of breath was she and John immediately towed her back to the exit that was only about six minutes away. On exiting John helped Cindy with her gear, and Cindy was too weak to get her hooded vest off at this point. Immediately when John helped Cindy remove her vest she was able to breathe normally, and after a few minutes Cindy recovered.

It was found that the new hooded dive vest Cindy had bought was so small that it constricted her chest so much as to not allow her to take even a normal breath, and she had to take short shallow breaths. In effect she was just pushing recycled air up and down as she could not ventilate her lungs properly, which resulted in her building up CO_2 rapidly. Thanks to John's attention to his buddy's breathing even though she was an instructor, and his decision to terminate the dive, a possible disaster was avoided, and a valuable lesson learned.

-Lessons from the above

Do not assume that your buddy can take care of himself or herself for any reason. They may be highly experienced, however factors not planned for can incapacitate them or affect their performance and decision-making ability. Although it is not needed to watch them like a hawk, an occasional check to make sure they are there and if they are behaving like normal should be OK. If anything is not going as normal, stop and see why.

Monitor your air supply frequently and ask your buddy every 500 psi of your consumption what theirs is. This way, you can note if their consumption changed or if they are low on gas. Furthermore, inform your buddy on how much you have. If you and your buddy have been diving together for a while, you should know to a reasonable accuracy what theirs is from your reading. If it is significantly different than expected, something is wrong, even if they give you the OK.

Furthermore, monitor your buddy's actual breathing rate by seeing how many breaths they take in a minute compared to you and how slowly they exhale on every breath. If the exhaled bubbles burst out with every breath, then they are exhaling too fast that will make it harder to breathe due to the gas becoming denser under water. In addition, check the time between breaths and the amount of bubbles exhaled to see how fast they breathe and how deeply.

Descend and ascend with your buddy next to you. If you drop like a stone to the bottom only looking down, how are you to know if your buddy is experiencing an emergency? On ascent, being with your buddy is not only cooler, but allows you to give assistance should any be needed. If you arrive at your safety stop or deco stop and your buddy is not there, you have a problem. Go find your wingman.

Chapter 18

Common mistakes made in deeper diving

Although there are many mistakes made by divers on any dive profile, here is a short list of some of the most common mistakes that can lead to serious injury or death.

1: Forgetting to turn the CCR unit on before entering the water.

2: Setting the incorrect gas on the dive computers before descending.

3: Not having tanks open on both CCR and OC before descending, this is normally more dangerous in CCR diving as the diver can have a hypoxic mixture without knowing it. An OC diver will notice if no gas can be had from a regulator; however the diver may panic and drown.

4: Breathing the wrong gas on descent or breathing a hypoxic mix too shallow.

5: Having the incorrect mixture in the CCR tanks (either due to accidently swapping the O2 and dill cylinder or not having the correct gas in the cylinders (diver did not analyze the gas)).

6: Ignoring low battery warnings on computers or CCR handsets on descent.

7: Switching to the incorrect mix at either the incorrect depth or time, leading to hypoxia, hyperoxia or incorrect decompression (including when bailing out on a CCR unit).

8: Losing a stage cylinder, normally due to clipping it off on to a wreck or line and not being able to return to the cyclinder.

9: Incorrectly calculating required gas volume, including not taking adequate bailout gas on a CCR unit.

10: Diving beyond your training.

11: Not following a continuous guide line in wrecks and caves.

12: Not taking enough or proper back up lights.

Chapter 19

Missed decompression

When things go wrong and a decompression stop is missed, there are a number of thoughts as to the procedure. Although this book is not meant as a deep diving training manual it is still a subject that should be glanced at.

The call for fast action is needed in order to prevent bubbles from forming in mass and to try and keep bubbles already formed from growing. The size of the bubbles plays a major role in decompression and recompression. The smaller the bubbles are, the faster they will dissolve. If recompression is done within 5 minutes, then it is normally adequate for treating bubbles of less than 100 micron in diameter. This is the basis for the Hawaiian emergency in-water recompression procedures, covered in the next chapter.

Missed stop

If the diver did not surface but only ascended past a stop, then the following procedures are normally followed. Note dive computers will track your decompression in real time, thus these suggestions are meant for dive tables or fixed dive plans. However, if you have a dive computer that displays decompression for each stop depth then you can note them on a slate and follow the suggestions below by increasing your deco using the calculations. Note, these are suggestions only; you are the diver and need to decide before the dive how you will handle an emergency.

-Return within a minute

If you can return to the missed stop depth within a minute, then do so and complete the stop and add a minute to the stop time. Add one minute run time to your bottom time or follow your next run time schedule or overrun schedule. You did create a backup plan for a three or five minute overrun time right?

-Return over one minute but within 5 minutes

If you cannot return to the missed stop within a minute, then return to the missed stop depth and do the required stop time according to your schedule. Multiply all stops 40 ft and shallower by 1.5 (or 2) and double your last stop. For example, if accidently missed an 80 ft two minute stop and returned in more than a minute to 80 ft, then complete two minutes at 80 ft. If your next stop was at 60 ft for five minutes then complete that as normal. If your next stops were 40 ft for 8 minutes, 30 ft for 10 minutes, 20 ft for 15 minutes and 15 ft for 25 minutes then you would do 12 minutes at 40 ft, 15 minutes at 30 ft, 23 minutes at 20 ft and 50 minutes at 15 ft.

-Not able to return to the missed stop

If you are not able to return to the missed stop but can stop at your next stop then do the combined time for both stops. For example, if you had two minutes at 80 ft that you missed and your next stop is five minutes at 60 ft, then do seven minutes at 60 ft. Extend all stops 40 ft and shallower the same as if you returned to the missed stop in over one minute.

In all cases, when you surface, breathe your highest Oxygen content gas for an additional five minutes or more if possible before you get out of the water. On the surface rest, drink plenty of water and monitor yourself for DCS. If you suspect DCS or are not sure about the dive, it will not hurt to breathe pure Oxygen.

Delay in ascent time

In some cases you might be delayed during your ascent and need to cater for it.

–Before reaching first stop

If you are delayed at the bottom or on your way up to your first stop then add the delay time to your bottom time and decompress on your overrun tables. Multiply your last stop by 1.5 or 2 if possible. If your delay exceeds your overrun tables extend all stops 40 ft and shallower by 1.5 (or 2).

–Delay between stops

If you are delayed between stops then it is a matter of where the delay was and for how long. A delay between your first and second stop or a delay at a deep depth can add a significant amount of decompression time to your schedule. If you are delayed between your first and second stop you can follow the same procedure as a delay before your first stop. If the delay is in the mid range stops and short (three to five minutes) then add the delay time to your last stop, if the delay is larger then multiply your last stop by 1.5 or 2. If the delay is at a shallow depth (40 ft and shallower) and small (around three to five minutes) then you can add that delay time to your last stop or increase the last stop by 1.5 to 2 times if the delay is more than 5 minutes.

Chapter 20

In water recompression

In water recompression (IWR) is a subject that most people either avoid or have a firm stance against. However, what is it all based on? This section should not be seen as a how to manual, it is only covered to make the reader aware of what has been and is being done in the diving field. As technical divers often dive in remote places, the chances are high that when things go wrong they have to fix it themselves.

Why not to do it

Since decompression sickness is not fully understood, nor its symptoms, placing a diver back in the water seems wrong. Not only may the diver on-gas additional inert gas, but if symptoms worsen the diver is at huge risk of drowning. The added inert gas dissolving into the tissues may make an already bad situation worse. IWR treatment normally requires long run times that can create problems because the environment may not support it (rough seas or weather, boat traffic, gas supply and thermal constraints). As the diver gets colder, off-gassing is reduced and the efficiency of the IWR attempt is reduced. If it is a neurological hit then the diver is at risk of going unconscious and possibly drowning, and even if not, the diver may be too tired to keep a regulator in the mouth. The diver may also be too weak to breathe against the added resistance of water pressure and a regulator.

Underwater it is also difficult to assess the diver's condition not to mention communicating with the diver. The increased inspired inert gas pressure will reduce the rate of inert gas elimination (may be a good thing to limit bubble growth but not always).

Even if pure O2 is used to limit inert gas on-gassing, there is still a risk of an O2 toxicity hit.

Why some do it

With DCS, time is critical, the longer treatment is delayed the more unlikely 100% resolution is. From investigations into DCS treatment and delay before treatment it was noted that if treatment is delayed beyond 6 hours then 100% resolution of symptoms is unlikely. This is one of the strongest reasons many people opt for IWR as symptoms (pain) may immediately be alleviated due to reducing the bubble size and the thought that since the bubble size is reduced and also possibly their formation, the risk of permanent damage to tissues is reduced while limiting the risk of tissue death due to tissue hypoxia.

Irreversible damage to nerve tissue can occur within 10 minutes of the initial hypoxic insult, thus the faster bubbles are compressed and decreased in size to allow blood flow to resume, the better. Since larger bubbles take longer to shrink and dissolve, the faster they are treated the faster DCS symptoms may disappear or be alleviated.

From research it was found that off-gassing when immersed in water is faster than when done in a dry chamber, thus shorter periods in water may have the same effect as a long chamber ride, if the diver is kept warm.

Types of IWR

There are many methods that are used for IWR, however three main practices are seen to be the most popular.

-Australian Method

Edmonds published an IWR method in the first edition of 'Diving and Subaquatic Medicine' (1976). It is suggested to provide O2 to the diver using a full face mask at a depth of 30 ft (9 m) for around 30-90 min depending on the symptoms. The diver is to then ascend at a rate of 1 ft/4 min (1 m/12 min). This method is now known as the "Australian Method".

Note that the dive can last up to three hours, thus plan for getting cold. A rescue diver should attend to the injured diver, and the injured diver will need a full face mask or helmet with O2. If symptoms recur on ascent remain at that depth for an additional 30 minutes before continuing the ascent. If O2 is insufficient, have the diver surface rather than breathe air at depth. After successfully completing the dive, the diver is to breathe surface O2 over an additional 12 hours one hour on, one hour off.

-U.S. Navy Method

In the 1985 U.S. Navy Diving Manual (Volume 1, revision 1,) an IWR procedure is given where a diver breathes O2 at 30 ft (9 m) for 60 min for pain only bends and 90 min for CNS DCS, followed by a 60 min stop at 20 ft (6 m) and a 60 min stop at 10 ft (3 m). After 90 minutes at 30 ft, the diver is to ascend to 20 ft even if symptoms are still present. On surfacing, breathe O2 for an additional three hours.

-Hawaiian method

Farm in 1986 gives a modification of the Australian Method for IWR. In this method the diver descends down to 30 ft (9 m) deeper than the depth where symptoms disappear for 10 minutes while breathing air (not to exceed 165 ft (50 m)).

The diver then ascends to 30 ft (9 m) where O2 is breathed for 60 minutes minimum followed by additional O2 breathing until symptoms disappear, emergency transport arrives, or the Oxygen supply is exhausted. This is known as the *"Hawaiian Method"*. Note, initial ascent from depth is 30 ft/minute with stops every minute for assessment of patient's condition with minimum ascent time being 10 minutes, suggested rates of ascents are 165 fsw initial ascent: 30 ft/minute x 2 minutes; 15 ft/minute x 2 minutes; 10 ft/minute x 3 minutes; 5 ft/minute x 3 minutes. Return to 10 ft deeper than current depth for 5 minutes if patient experiences recurring symptoms.

Additional suggestions

Following are additional suggestions that are combinations of different sources for omitted decompression upon surfacing.

-20 ft (6 m) or shallower

If you surface without completing your decompression for a depth not exceeding 20 ft (6 m) and have no symptoms of DCI, then return to your depth and complete the missed stop times. Extend your last stop time by 1.5 or 2 times, especially if your return time is more than one minute. Upon resurfacing breathe O2 for around an hour or as long as possible (highest deco mix will also do) and monitor for symptoms while drinking plenty of water.

–Deeper than 20 ft (6 m)

If you surfaced and missed your stops from a depth deeper than 20 ft (6 m) and have no symptoms of DCI then return to the deepest stop depth you missed (within five minutes preferred). Do all stops deeper than 40 ft as normal, then increase all stops 40 ft and shallower by 1.5 or 2 times.

As before, in all cases when returning to the surface, breathe O2 for at least an hour if possible or your highest deco mix. Drink plenty of water, refrain from exercise and monitor for symptoms and signs of DCS.

IWR attempt investigated

A study was done on 535 cases of attempted IWR to see the effectiveness of IWR. In 527 cases complete resolution of symptoms was found as an end result, however 51 cases were reported in the diver surfacing with residual symptoms mild enough that the diver did not seek further treatment and residual symptoms were reported to have disappeared entirely within a day or two.

In 14 cases the diver surfaced with residual symptoms that had the diver seek treatment at a recompression facility. It should be noted that none of the divers reported their symptoms worsened during or after IWR.

Anton Swanepoel

One would then wonder what procedure these divers followed, the shocking discovery is that none of the divers were aware of any published or official IWR method and just planned it on the way down and all used air and not O2 for recompression. Very much like singing deep stops (stop at half your max depth and sing some songs depending on how much you trust the deco schedule).

There have been reports of divers using the Australian method with tremendous success, and other cases of divers using dive computers to plan the IWR with some success. However, an additional twenty cases after the report were reported which contained two cases that resulted in the death of the divers (both divers were together at the time), and in one case a sore shoulder resulted in the diver becoming a permanent quadriplegic.

It is possible that many more cases exist as IWR is often done in remote places and divers do not always talk about it, in addition to professional divers not wanting to place their work in jeopardy (in a private review many confirmed that they have used IWR to treat both themselves and companions on multiple occasions with great success).

Case example

Two different cases will be looked at to give an example of how unclear IWR is.

Case 1:
Four fishermen were working in Hawaii to depths of around 165 to 180 ft with each making two dives. Two divers rapidly developed CNS DCS upon surfacing from the second dive. The boat immediately headed for the dock about 30 minutes away where a recompression chamber could be reached within an hour. However, one diver elected to rather do IWR, and taking two full scuba tanks entered the water to around 30 to 40 ft. When the boat returned two hours later he was asymptomatic and apparently cured, however the other diver died of severe DCS in the Med-Evac helicopter while on the way to the recompression chamber.

Case 2:
Twelve divers made a dive to around 215 ft in Sussex, England on a wreck. Upon surfacing, two of the divers reported that they missed their decompression.

Both divers decided to do IWR and returned to the water after obtaining additional air tanks. Both never surfaced and their bodies were found two weeks later. The reason as to their death is unclear.

Conclusion

In water recompression is a very difficult subject, and although it is practiced by some military agencies, it is normally done with extensive support, O2 and full face masks. Due to the large risk associated with IWR it is understandable that governing bodies would not advocate it, however the large success rate cannot be overlooked, and for a technical diver far removed from a recompression chamber it may be a viable option. However, it is a decision the diver needs to make alone while knowing the risks of possibly increasing the problem, becoming paraplegic, and possibly drowning.

Divers should note that often symptoms disappear if O2 is breathed on the surface (bubbles shrink 10 times faster when breathing O2) and that if this is the case IWR is often not needed or advised. Should symptoms persist when O2 is breathed on the surface and a recompression chamber is not within easy reach, then IWR is an option and perhaps should be attempted if the diver is of sound mind and physically capable of doing the dive. Note however that since high partial pressures of O2 would be breathed, it is advised that the diver take five minute air breaks every 20 minutes on O2.

Final note on IWR

This chapter is not to advocate IWR, but to show IWR as a possibility that should be further investigated, and also to make the reader aware that it is being done with success and failure, as is decompression diving at the moment. Thus both carry risk that only the diver can decide if it is worth it.

Chapter 21

Liquid breathing

When one talks about liquid breathing for diving, the movie 'The Abyss' comes to mind. One might think that reaching 10 000 ft breathing an Oxygenated liquid is only for the movies, however it is more real than people think. Every person on this planet that was conceived in the womb has breathed liquid in their life.

Although a fetus gets all the Oxygen it needs from the umbilical cord, practice breathing by inhaling and exhaling amniotic fluid is done in the later stages of gestation thought to be important to fetal lung development.

The first test of liquid breathing was in saline solutions, but failed due to the saline solution not being able to remove adequate quantities of CO_2 from the body.

In 1966, Clark and Gollan started experimenting with perfluorocabons (PFC) and submerged mice in the Oxygenated liquid for a time with successful return to normal breathing after removal. Liquid breathing using perfluorocabons (made of mostly fluorine and carbon) is possible due to the liquid having ¼ the surface tension, 16 times the O2 solubility and three times the CO2 solubility of water. Liquid breathing may be thought of only useful for scientific, military and deep diving, however it has a useful role in medical applications as well.

Oxygenated liquid breathing can be used for respiratory disorders and may assist the over 80,000 premature newborns delivered each year with severe respiratory disorders. Liquid breathing can deliver more O2 easier than supplemental O2 breathing. The liquid can also be used for adult patients who experience breathing distress or have chronic obstructive pulmonary disease.

By the mid-1990s, Professor Thomas Shaffer and a handful of doctors started using liquid ventilation techniques on premature babies with excellent results. Professor Shaffer notes that many of the babies have only around a 5% chance of survival without treatment, however with liquid breathing almost 60% are able to lead normal lives. Even though the results are impressive, liquid breathing for infants remains rare due to lack of investment.

The best liquid in use today is perflubron (also known as 'LiquiVent') and is a clear liquid with twice the density of water, double the O2 capacity per unit of volume as air while being inert. The liquid has a very low boiling point and can be cleared from the lungs easily by evaporation.

For deep diving liquid breathing has some distinct advantages over gas breathing due to no gas phase coming in contact with blood and no N2 being used in liquid breathing. Thus DCS risk is basically eliminated. From tests done on rats in the 1960s, it was observed that rats survive for up to 20 hours while breathing liquid. Professor Shaffer has done tests on mice up to 1000 ft depth and then decompressed them in ½ a second with no DCS incidence.

It is reported that the Navy Seals experimented with liquid breathing and in the cases had divers dive multiple times a week. Due to the stress of getting the liquid into and out of the lungs some divers developed stress fractures on the ribs. For deep diving, a device called a cuirass (named after a piece of medieval armor) may be used for ventilation. The device compresses the diaphragm to assist in breathing and can make liquid breathing easier. This is due to the density of liquid being too much for a diver to cope with alone for extended periods as the diaphragm muscles are not used to that resistance.

A different method may also be used with total liquid ventilation (TLV) devices. Here the system artificially induces respiration for the diver, almost like artificial respirators used in hospitals. Tubes may be inserted into the diver's lungs and the unit may pump a steady flow of Oxygenated liquid into the lungs. Flow rate may be adjusted to compensate for diver exertion level. A special CO_2 filter would then filter the liquid while O2 is replenished into the liquid from a reserve canister, almost like a liquid CCR unit. Drugs may be used to suppress a diver's gag and panic reflexes.

Originally it was thought that liquid breathing can allow a diver to descend to depths of around 3 000 ft (914 m); however it is now thought that it may be possible to reach 10 000 ft – tomorrow may bring what yesterday was thought impossible.

Is our depth unlimited?

It may seem that breathing liquid allows us to go to unlimited depths, but this may not be the case. From studies done on frogs by Harvey and coworkers, it was found that cells were paralyzed between 1650 and 4950 ft (500 and 1500 m) and that damage was irreversible at between 8250 and 9900 ft (2500 and 3000 m). At these pressures the cells contract, the nucleus becomes pyknotic (a thickening degeneration of the cell that the nucleus shrinks in size and the chromatin condenses to a solid) and the cytoplasm (a gel-like substance residing between the cell membrane holding all the cell's internal sub-structures and where all cell active occurs) fills with vacuoles (enclosed compartments filled with water).

Proteins were also found to coagulate from around 165 000 ft (50 000 m) and enzyme activity stops at around 396 000 ft (120 000 m). Life at greater pressures has been found in the ocean and the question is how did they adapt to these pressures?

An interesting observation was made when goats were held at 41 ata (1320 ft, 400 m) with a PPO2 of 0.2 and then taken to 58 ata (1881 ft, 570 m). The goats showed signs of hypoxia at pressures over 41 ata on a PPO2 of 0.2 until the PPO2 was raised to 0.4 (hypoxia symptoms reappeared if the PPO2 was lowered gain). It is thought that a decrease in the gaseous pulmonary exchange occurs due to the pressure.

Other uses for liquid breathing

Although Shaffer saves lives with his work on premature babies, there are other uses for liquid breathing than deep diving and saving premature babies' lives.

-Cardiac arrest

Currently, the expectancy of surviving a cardiac arrest is around one in 20; with a new technique it is thought that survival could be as high as one in three.

Dr. Peter Safar (who introduced CPR to the US) doing research in his lab at the University of Pittsburgh Medical Center started looking into liquid cooling the lungs in order to cool the body. The reason is that when cardiac death occurs at normal body temperature, permanent brain damage occurs after five minutes. With no blood flowing to the brain, cells exhaust their O2 within 10 seconds and unconsciousness results. Within five minutes glucose reserves are used up and cells start to poison themselves.

Safar however discovered in his experiments (in the 1980s) that the five minute time can be doubled with mild hypothermia. Thus survival time of cardiac arrest could be extended to 10 minutes. The problem however was how to quickly cool a patient while in the field.

Perfluorocarbons came on the scene and a new idea was born where the liquid (chilled) can be pumped into the patient's lungs with Oxygen. The liquid will then supply a greater amount of Oxygen to the lungs (due to the liquid being able to hold more Oxygen) while rapidly cooling the lungs and body.

As manual heart massage is done (or if the heart is restarted with a defibrillator), the blood that flows then to the brain will be cooled, cooling the brain and extending the life of the brain cells. Michael Darwin and Steven Harris started research on a prototype unit and in 1999 created a sensation when they made a preliminary announcement at a medical conference.

Darwin and Harris were able to cool the subjects three times faster than other researchers, with a cooling in blood temperature of 14 °F (57.2 °C) and a brain temperature cooling of 13.3 °F (55.94 °C) in 18 minutes. Harris and Darwin then proceeded to develop and test a device than can deliver cooled perfluorocarbon in the field.

This module can be loaded into emergency personnel vehicles responding to emergency calls. The cooled liquid will be pumped through a tube in and out of the patient's lungs automatically about every 30 seconds with a sensor in the eardrum that keeps track of the blood temperature. Currently the device is undergoing more testing, however the research has attracted other larger research organizations and it is estimated that over 100,000 lives a year may be saved by such a device.

-Space travel

Liquid breathing may allow us to travel faster in space by reducing the effects of g-force on the body. Due to forces applied to fluids being distributed omnidirectionally and due to liquids not practically being compressible, their density changes little with high acceleration forces.

By immersing a person in a liquid with the same density as body tissue, acceleration forces are now distributed around the body and not on single points. This allows individuals to cope with higher total g-force and is currently used by aircraft pilots using a new suit, called the Libelle G-suit, which allows pilots to remain conscious at more than 10 G acceleration force. 1 G is equal to the gravitational force of the earth.

However, the suit has a limit of around 15 to 20 G due to different densities between the body tissues and immersion fluid. If the lungs however are filled with a liquid while the body is immersed in liquid, then little pressure effect will be felt by a person and the G-force limit can drastically be increased. This is actually the main concept of using liquid breathing for deep dives as the body will already be surrounded by water, no suit or tie required. ☺

Chapter 22

Deep diving records

So what really is deep then? Many people think that 100 ft is deep, while others consider 300 ft to be deep, yet from the introduction we have seen that seals can dive to almost 5000 ft. Thus depth is just a number and deep diving is relevant only to the observer.

Following are a number of deep diving achievements that may humble us a bit. Note depth conversion from feet to meters is calculated at 3.3 ft for 1 m.

Although not deep, the longest salt water scuba dive is 82,5 hours, UShaka Marine World Durban South Africa, December 2004.

5 cm (2 inches) depth of water you can drown in
73 cm (2.5 ft) depth from which a lung over expansion injury can occur.
7 m (23 ft) max depth one is thought to be able to ascend directly to the surface while being saturated, without DCS forming.
12 m (40 ft) max depth for a junior PADI Open Water diver
18 m (60 ft) max depth for a PADI Open Water diver
20 m (66 ft) max depth coral is thought to be able to grow (depending on light level)
30 m (100 ft) max depth for a PADI Advanced diver
40 m (130 ft) max recreational depth
50 m (165 ft) max depth for a PADI DSAT Tech deep diver (air)
54 m (180 ft) max depth for IANTD and TDI deep air diving
60 m (200 ft) maximum depth for normoxic Tri-Mix diving (contains a normal O2 amount in the mix, 20%)
66 m (218 ft) depth that O2 in air reaches 1.6 ata
100 m (330 ft) deepest depth for normal Tri-Mix dive training
121 m (400 ft) deepest non commercial certification obtainable (expedition Tri-Mix from IANTD)

155 m (509 ft) deepest air dive, 1994 Dan Manion
159 m (524.7 ft) deepest woman wreck dive, Mayday 2007, Nina Preisner, wreck of the Jolanda
160 m (528 ft) deepest female freedive, Tanya Streeter, 17 August 2002
200 m (660 ft) limit that surface light is able to penetrate that is sufficient for plant growth
205 m (672 ft) deepest wreck dive, December 12, 2005, Leigh Cunningham and Mark Andrews, wreck of the MV Yolande
214m (706 ft) deepest male freedive, Herbert Nitsch, Austria, 14 June 2007

270 m (885 ft) deepest cave CCR dive, Dave Shaw, October 28, 2004 , modified Mk 15.5 rebreather, Boesmansgat, South Africa

282.6m (933 ft) deepest cave dive, Nuno Gomes, Boesmansgat, South Africa

330 m (1083 ft) deepest OC dive, Pascal Bernabé (Ralf Tech/WR1 Team), July 5, 2005, Propriano, Corsica (unassisted descent)

347.87 m (1148 ft) deepest OC open ocean dive, June 1975, British Royal Navy diver William Rhodes, Gulf of Mexico. Four divers were taken down in a transfer chamber to 1000 ft where they then went deeper on their own

438.91 m (1440 ft) deepest Jim suit dive, 1976, Spain (to recover a TV cable)

606.06 m (2000 ft) deepest Atmospheric Diving System (ADS) dive, US Navy, off the coast of La Jolla, California, August 1, 2007. At this depth one has access to only about 10% of the ocean floor

701 m (2313 ft) deepest recorded saturation dive

1020m (3366 ft) deepest military operating submarine

1515.15 m (5000 ft) deepest depth man is thought to be able to breathe compressed gas, from experimental chamber exposure at the University of Pennsylvania

2424.24 m (8000 ft) deepest recorded depth from research that large animals have been exposed to and safely brought to the surface, although current testing may have exceeded this depth already

3000m (9900 ft) deepest depth for a sperm whale

3030.3 m (10 000 ft) deepest depth a human is thought to be able to dive and swim freely around. The diver would be breathing an Oxygenated liquid

3810m (12 573 ft) final resting place of the RMS Titanic

5606m (18 500 ft) deepest point in the Arctic ocean, Molloy Deep

5762m (19 015 ft) deepest shipwreck discovered

6000m (19 800 ft) deepest depth of the Russian Mir submersible

6500m (21 450 ft) deepest depth of the Japanese Shinkai submersible

7235m (23 876 ft) deepest point in the Southern Ocean, South Sandwich Trench

8047m (26 555 ft) deepest point in the Indian Ocean, Diamantina Trench

8380m (27 654 ft) deepest point in the Atlantic Ocean, Puerto Rico Trench

8848m (29 198 ft) height of Mt Everest

10,911 m (35,797 ft) deepest depth the Trieste, a deep-diving research vessel reached, Challenger Deep, Mariana Trench near Guam, 23 January 1960

11034m (36 412 ft) deepest unexplored point on the planet, Pacific Ocean, Mariana trench

11212m (37 000 ft) deepest operating submarine, Virgin Oceanic submarine

How deep have you gone lately? ☺

End Note

Thank you for your purchase of this book. May it be a constant companion and an old friend on your journeys.

For comments please e-mail me at info@antonswanepoelbooks.com

Anton Swanepoel

Resources

Books:
Technical Diving
Technical Diving From The Bottom Up
Technical Diving Encyclopedia
Diving Physiology In Plain English
Deep Deeper Deepest
Mixed Gas Diving
Exploration And Mixed Gas Diving
Deeper Diving

Articles:
28 February 1994, The DSAT Recreational Dive Planner

People:
Charlie Christensen
Russell Lait

Spelling and grammar:
Toni McNally
Ginger It! Spelling and grammar Software
WhiteSmoke spelling and grammar software

Internet websites:
http://jap.physiology.org
http://pages.uoregon.edu/lovering/lab/index.html
http://discovermagazine.com
http://www.livestrong.com
http://en.wikipedia.org
http://www.scuba-doc.com
http://www.diversalertnetwork.org/
http://www.cavediver.net
http://www.thefullwiki.org
http://www.southpacificdivers.com
http://technical-sidemount.com
http://www.scubamonster.com
http://plongee-tech.pagesperso-orange.fr
http://retis.sssup.it
http://ajwatts.co.uk
http://www.direxplorers.com
http://www.pure-tech-agency.net
http://www.cognitas.org.uk

Anton Swanepoel

http://rubicon-foundation.org
http://jap.physiology.org
http://pages.uoregon.edu/lovering/lab/index.html
http://www.jmvh.org

Workshops
The Physiological Basis of Decompression (Undersea Hyperbaric Medical Society) Proceeding 38
Biomechanics of Safe Ascents (American Academy of Underwater Science, 1989)

Other Books by this Author

For a complete list of books by the author and more details on each book see
www.antonswanepoelbooks.com/books.php

The Art of Gas Blending
www.antonswanepoelbooks.com/the_art_of_gas_blending.php

This is an excellent must have book for any gas blender, Technical diver or person interested in technical diving, whether you intend to blend gas or not.

Taking on the Road, Two Wheels at a Time
www.antonswanepoelbooks.com/taking_on_the_road.php

Traveling by motorcycle is far different than any other means of transport. In a car, you are always a passenger, seeing a movie of the road going by. On a bike you become one with it, the road and your surrounding is no longer a movie, it's a part of you. For you feel every corner, every bump and your body flexes in harmony with the bike's suspension. You smell the flowers, earth and rain, feel the wind and hear birds as you go, *you are alive.*

This book aims to help you prepare for your next adventure or your first, from down to the pub races, breakfast runs, multiple weeklong rallies, or yearlong multi country travel. From gear selection, packing right, understanding your bike and setting the suspension right to maintenance on the road.

The Art of Travel
www.antonswanepoelbooks.com/the_art_of_travel.php

Travelling is more than just reaching your destination; it's the journey in its totality. Travel is about growing as a person.

Pre-planning, gear selection, backpacks, tents, sleeping bags, boots, clothing, flashlights, GPS devices, pickpocketing, robbery, abduction, date rape drugs, protecting your food in the wild, keeping the crawlers out of your sleeping bag at night, and tips to help you with sticky situations along the way, are all covered in depth.

New adventures and friends are out there, what are you waiting for?

Gas Blender Program

www.antonswanepoelbooks.com/gas_blender_program.php

A step by step guide to creating your own gas blender program in Excel.

This book will show you how to write a blender program in Excel step by step with the values needed for every cell and function. No need to be a programmer, just type in the values from each step.

The program will run on most devices that support spreadsheets, from computers, laptops, smart phones, palms, and iPhones.
Calculations for Nitrox, Tri-Mix, Helair, Heliox, EAD and END are covered, in addition to calculations for actual rebreather loop at depth and END included.

Dive Computers

www.antonswanepoelbooks.com/dive_computers.php

The purpose and aim of this book is to help you in understanding how dive computers work, including calculations on decompression stops, deep stops, ascend ceilings, on- and off gassing, RGBM, VPM and gradient factors.

Sea and Motion Sickness

http://www.antonswanepoelbooks.com/motion_sickness.php

In this book, we will look at what motion sickness is, space sickness, virtual environment sickness, and sea sickness, their causes and triggers, with advice for preventing and treating them. Included in the book is ginger, antihistamine medication, wrist bands, natural herbs, behavior adaption and a lot more, all helping you travel without motion sickness.

Ear Pain

http://www.antonswanepoelbooks.com/ear_pain.php

There are a few different causes of ear pain, and the treatment for each may differ. Understanding why your ears hurt is the first step in finding the off switch to the pain and preventing it from coming on again. Some of the topics covered are: ear pain due to barotrauma, swimmer's ear, surfer's ear, jogging and waterskiing, cold in the ear, airplane ear, ear infection, Tinnitus and referred pain from a tooth abscess. From causes, prevention, to treatment in detail. Additional included is over 10 ways to equalize your ears.

Writing and Publishing Your Own Book

http://www.antonswanepoelbooks.com/writing_and_publishing.php

Change your words from '*I am going*', to '*I have written a book*'
You can be a writer, for it's a skill learnable by most people. Being a writer is not only a dream for the select few, it's within most people's ability.
In this book I will show you the steps to start and finish writing your book, including publishing and selling it. If you already have books written, you can use the tips to enhance old books and improve future books.

Deep and safety Stops, including Ascent speed and Gradient Factors

http://www.antonswanepoelbooks.com/deepstops.php

This book looks at the research done and current understandings of deep stops, both for and against deep stops. The book's aim is not to advocate or discredit the use of deep stops, but rather to be neutral and provide the reader with the most up to date knowledge, research and methods used by various groups, from military to recreational diving. The reader is shown the risks of both incorporating deep stops or not into their dive profile and it is up to the reader to decide if using deep stops is of any benefit in addition to how if any the user will calculate and execute those stops.

This book also looks at safety stops, ascent speed, descent speed, oxygen window and gradient factors and how they affect your decompression schedule

See www.antonswanepoelbooks.com for more details.

Made in the USA
San Bernardino, CA
24 January 2014